Before my coat of skin

Naked

Love, Life, Religion, God

By Gina Genelle

All Scripture and biblical quotations have been taken from the King James Version of the Bible, unless otherwise indicated.

Naked

by Gina Genelle

Before my coat of skin

One woman's passage to attain knowledge and understanding of love, life, religion and a real God

Design and Editing by Gina Genelle © 2010/2014 by Gina G. Miller D.V.8 Publishing Co, LLC

All rights reserved under National Copyright Law. No part of this book, content, and/or cover may be reproduced or transmitted in any form in whole or in part by any means without the express written permission from the author.

"Be not conformed to the things of the world, but be transformed by the renewing of your mind"

DEVIATE

Foreword

In the beginning... The beginning of what?

Who is it that bestows these truths? Who is it that is fit to validate life and govern proofs, other than you? Who is it that sets the tone for life, if it is indeed your life and yours alone? Who is to sets the eminence for your growth and maturity, and to what degree, and if not you, than who? Are you then truly measured as free?

Who is it that is qualified to utter my thinking and ideal, and to whose appeal or partiality? Who is he that has written our reality, forcing us to at times wire walk the bounds of insanity, chase vanity as if it were the Father, the most High?

At what point are we entitled to realize our true God given nature and ability and be free? These are the things I continue to ask me.

Why me? Because it is I that I truly trust, and must study to show myself approved. Developing my own rationale, my raison d'être, my Way, my will to be free... the existent Genesis of me.

Truth has always been both painful and liberating. It allows one to recognize the things that are true about themselves.

Truth has possessed the ability to free one from the struggle of mental concealment. Accepting truth will allow a person an opportunity to change certain aspects of them, if they have found their truth to be unacceptable. I simply call the acceptance of truth, the highest form of repentance. How else can a person be Godly sorry for wrongdoing if they have refused to accept that wrongdoing is a natural part of them?

I have, on many occasions, found myself repenting for things about me that I love. I have found myself not accepting my life, fearful that it would offend someone else.

I realize that the truth about my life involves individuals who are unwilling or even unable to accept truth. Regardless of the involvement of others, I am entitled to accept truth my personal truth.

I battled with the idea of how to classify this book. I was concerned about what people may say or feel. I was concerned for the anger that certain individuals would

express. Simply put, it is either fiction or non-fiction. To the individuals who feel as if the things written in this book are not true, then the book is fiction and they should not have a problem. For those who feel that it is true, than it is non-fiction, and this opportunity should be taken to do an overall self-examination prior to passing judgment on me or my views of my life's journey. To me, it is my life, my experiences, my account of reality.

I would like to apologize in advance to anyone who may be offended. It is not my intent to cause harm or discomfort, nor is it my intent to discredit or slander anyone, anyone's beliefs or their practices. If you feel that you will be angry after reading this book, it is my advice that you put the book down now before absorbing its content. You have the choice not to read it. I am going to tell it like I see it. If your views of things were and are different, I would encourage you to write a book, just as I have.

Preface

The core of my existence has been based on the views and precepts of those who study and conclude based on their own invention and discovery. I am now seizing the same opportunity and ability to do the same for my self-preservation as well as that of my legacy.

The reason I say "my" existence, is that I enclose to be cautious not to speak for anyone but myself, in efforts to avoid offending anyone's principle or certainty.

It is my intent to express my thoughts and credence, and share them with the world, with the understanding that I will be criticized, demoralized, and even set aside. My hopes are of touching those who have and are partakers of a similar life's journey, traveling in anticipation of reaching a final kismet or measure of understanding.

I know that I will be asked, "Who do you think you are?" but the question should always be, "Who do you say that I am? For it is the prerogative of the questioner to decide who I am to them. For we have not the authority to think for anyone but ourselves. This is truly the power of a sound mind.

With those things being said, I will only request of the Most High God, on your behalf that understanding is received while reading the content of this exchange of ideas. That this Word be accepted as rations for mental and spiritual resurgence, for the benefit of the edification of the Body. Let he who has an ear, hear...

All thanks to the ineffable

Ehyeh Asher Ehyeh

I AM that I AM

Unto Adam also and to his wife did the LORD God make coats of skins, and clothed them.

Gen 3:21

This book is dedicated to

Sharhonda and Rahni

There is no attainable thought of life without the two of you. You are my life, my love, my religion, my path to finding the ineffable.

If ever there were a choice for life, these would be mine.

My beautiful daughters

Also…

Mildred Miller, Sharhonda Armstead, Effie Miller & Eva Mae Fulcher

My guardian Angels

TABLE OF CONTENTS

Foreword

Preface

Page 1   **Chapter 1**

GENESIS

Page 3	I remember a time
Page 11	The change in atmosphere
Page 21	Not all misery loves company

Page 27   **Chapter 2**

LOL... CHURCH!

Page 29	I may have mistaken emotion for the spirit of God
Page 43	And the morning and the evening were the first day

Page 49   **Chapter 3**

AND YE SHALL SURELY DIE

Page 51	She would still be alive had you told someone
Page 61	My trial and some tribulations began

Page 65	**Chapter 4**

ADAM WHERE ARE YOU?

Page 67	Where was I?
Page 79	**Chapter 5**

THE SHORT OF THE LONG OF IT

Page 81	Stone Cold
Page 91	Free spirited
Page 95	I don't remember asking for that
Page 99	Crack kills
Page 103	Page New Jack itty-bitty city
Page 115	**Chapter 6**

CHAPTER ONE, VERSE ONE

Page 117	They spelled her name wrong
Page 121	A POEM CALLED TRUTH
Page 129	**Chapter 7**

THE BEGINNING OF A NEW END

Page 131	An old-fashioned mess
Page 135	I'm pretty sure nothing good comes from the hood

Page 147	Time to put my face on
Page 151	Old Chester the molester was back, just in new skin
Page 155	My demonic possession
Page 159	Things were getting out of hand
Page 165	Prom nightmare
Page 169	I mean no harm
Page 179	A POEM CALLED NAKED
Page 183	**Chapter 8**

BEFORE THE FALL

Page 185	Why is our good always evil spoken of
Page 193	**Chapter 9**

LIFE AND LOVE, OR SO IT'S CALLED

Page 195	On my own again
Page 199	I graduated
Page 203	Turned on by the idea of love short lived
Page 209	Don't go breaking my heart
Page 211	A POEM CALLED FOR YOU I WILL
Page 215	The tie that binds
Page 221	What I must do to really love and be loved

	again
Page 223	A POEM CALLED HUMBLED
Page 231	Chapter 10

GOT ME LOOKING LIKE GOMER PYLE

Page 233	U.S. ARMY (Uncle Sam Ain't Released Me Yet)
Page 239	No peace in a time of war
Page 251	A POEM CALLED IN HIS IMAGE AND LIKENESS
Page 255	**Chapter 11**

god or GOD?

Page 257	DV8 (Deviate)
Page 285	**Chapter 12**

Naked

Page 297	Proverbial Evolution/Taking the Blame for my own fall
Page 299	Proverbial Evolution

GENESIS

Chapter 1

I REMEMBER A TIME

I can remember vividly, being between the first and second pews of the sanctuary. My hands were firmly gripping the top of the pew in front of me to the extent of my reach. I held on tightly in efforts to maintain my balance as I jumped up and down to the sound of what we called shout music. Shouting to most people is to utter words in a loud voice, but in the black enthusiastic Apostolic, Pentecostal, Holiness church...shouting was performing the Holy dance that would get you right into heaven without passing go, or collecting your two hundred dollars. The church was hype, and folk were jumping everywhere. And I, little Gina, was getting my shout on.

I was with my great grandmother, whom I to this day and in her absence, I still adore her. She is my watcher. She was a very tall light, bright, damn near white skinned woman with long curly salt and pepper hair. It was years before I knew she was actually white. I thought she just had pale skin. The tenor of her voice reigned profoundly, sultry as I remember it. She was the type of woman who would be quick to slap your face if you were ever deemed disrespectful or out of line, regardless of your age. I have to laugh because I remember her slapping my mother for talking out of turn. She loved God, and was adamant about having the uncontested truth. She was saved and would not tolerate anyone who was not willing to conform to her truth.

I remember on this particular Sunday morning, the slight touch of an elderly woman's hand, touching mine as she conversed with my great grandmother. They were admiring the effort that I put into praising God. Trying to impress them, I began to shout harder and knocked my head so hard on the wooden portion of the pew that I was holding to keep my balance. Holding in my cry, I tried not to disturb their admiration of my worship.

I believe this to be my very first memory of my life. It is also all that I remember of that day, that one moment. My beginning...

It amazes me that my life's very first memory is one of me praising God. And Although I am sure that I had not a clear understanding of what was going on, I must have felt that it was the right thing to do. I give these memories to set the stage for what is to come. I will try to remain on track, but in all actuality, I am a pretty sporadic individual. So bear with me, I will try and keep it interesting.

In all my remembering, I have stronger memories of my mother, I viewed her as being the most beautiful creature to be formed. I can remember feeling her spirit as she sang the words, "God's woman, that's what I want to be, for all the world to see, His woman." I was in love with her love for this God that she spoke, prayed, and would sing to. The same God that I assume I was admired for praising in the sanctuary with my great grandmother that one Sunday morning.

This would probably explain why I praised. I would have learned it from my mother's constant worship and reverence for Him, God.

My actions were more than likely an imitation of my mother's constant worship at home. I was more than likely reenacting what I saw. I was an exact duplicate, replicating her mannerism to the point of allowing others to feel my praise as I felt my mother's praise. Maybe they were feeling her praise through me. Maybe I had only been a vessel. Maybe I was a vessel unto Him, the very same God that she spoke with prior to us leaving the house, asking him to keep us safe, to allow His angels to encamp themselves around and about us, keeping us safe from all hurt harm and danger, asking Him to bind any evil adversary that would attempt to come against us.

She would also speak to this God before we ate dinner, asking him to purify our meals and to bless them for our nourishment and would thank Him for the provisions.

The very same God that she would speak to before we went to bed, requesting that He keeps us covered under His precious anointing. The God she cried to when the woes of life would trouble her spirit. Surely, this guy was powerful. Whoever He was, I couldn't wait to meet Him. I thought He must have been my father because I had never seen him at the time. I would always try to put a face with the name, assuming that someone passing me could quite possibly be God. I continued searching for Him.

These were my thoughts as a child. I thought God was a man I had not met. I did not quite understand the principle of God, but recognized his magnitude.

I can dimly recall, my mother, having a headache and asking me to pray for her. I remember placing my tiny fingertips in the core of her brow, rubbing what she called blessed oil on her. This was Extra Virgin Olive Oil that had been prayed over by the pastor and other ministers in the church. I remember asking her God to take away her headache and to rebuke the devil, mimicking the tone and character of our pastor while praying. Shortly after the prayer, I remember her telling me that she had been healed and thanking me for my prayer. I'm sure she remained in pain, but knowing my mother, she was telling the truth, I have never known her to lie and she was very big on faith.

As I smiled, turgid with pride, I knew that as she trusted God, she trusted me to trust God for her. I had no real discernment of what was really happening, but knew for certain there was power in prayer associated with the name of a man she called Jesus. I understood that he was the son of God. This must have meant I had a step brother because I truly believed God was my father. Each time she would pray to God, she would pray in this name. She would constantly tell me that there was power in that name.

Although I didn't appreciate the degree of that power then, it is something that I have held near for the whole of my life, unwavering incessantly. It is not so much the name, but my faith in knowing that the name carries power because of whom and what it represents, regardless of a title.

THE CHANGE IN ATMOSPHERE

My mother moved us into another town and the very thread of her essence began to shift. It was as if the woman I once knew was no more. I could not understand what was happening. She began to smoke cigarettes and drink beer. She entertained strange men and it was less often that I would hear of her God, with exception of always praying in the New Year without fail.

I would at times call out to her and receive no response. She was too busy with her newfound refuge.

As the situation would have it, the change was very reminiscent of knocking my head on the pew as a younger child. One minute I was praising God, the next, I cannot recall or even make clear the whys of so much pain. I could not understand why I would ignore that same pain for the sake of someone's approval of my efforts.

These precious memories stain the foundation of my origin as I identify it today. Accounts that are in keeping with the order of my life's developments be they fine or dire, nevertheless purpose! They have cultivated my way of thinking and believing based on the series of events that were derivative of the consistent drastic change in atmosphere.

Years came, went, and times waxed worse for me. I lacked love and affection. Those things had been replaced with being unseen by my mom and molested[1] by a family member who convinced me to believe that I asked for it. I had no clue of what it was that I asked for be still accepted the responsibility, asking God to make me aware of when I would request such happenings. He was the first but not the last.

---

[1] I have to make clear the meaning of molestation, I was not raped. Molestation is to be subjected to unwanted or improper sexual advances. I was being inappropriately touched in a sexual manner by an adult male with his hands and penis. No sexual intercourse took place.

After telling, I remember being told that we do not get family in trouble or that I provoked it. I was confused and did not understand. The only thing I knew in my mind was that it was not right nor was it love. I wanted it to stop and I was afraid. I knew that I needed to protect my younger sisters from it, even if that meant accepting it. I thought if I continued to allow it, the men would have no need for my sisters. I sacrificed myself in a sense

I spent many nights trying to recall the moment I asked to be violated. Innocent could never be an excuse for me, I was perceived to be intellectually inclined as a child. For that reason, no one was to come to my rescue. It was alleged that I was encouraging these happenings and I was treated as if I was to take some responsibility for being taken advantage of by someone, an adult. I was accused of lying about it all. Little did they know, I was a virgin and the only introduction to anything sexual in nature, was presented to me during an assembly in elementary school. By this time, I had already been molested several times.

During this assembly, it was vividly explained to me that being touch inappropriately was wrong. It was then that I realized that I should tell someone. I did.

When my great grandmother, whom I lived with at the time, was called to the school, she explained to the counselor that the man who had allegedly molested me was recently murdered. This same man had held my mother and all of us children against our will years prior. Ironically, he had the same first name as my cousin who had actually molested me. My great grandmother and I both knew my cousin had done the damage. It was not the dead man my die-hard Christian great grandmother had blamed to protect family.

We left the school making no mention ever again, of what had taken place, nor the fact that my cousin molested me. I left there feeling as if I was wrong for telling on my family. I was afraid that she would stop loving me. She never did stop loving me. She carried on as if the situation never took place, keeping me carefully guarded. The molestation never stopped. The men just changed. I never told again.

I experienced the same issues while serving as a Soldier. Instead of acknowledging that I was the victim, a full investigation was launched against me, after reporting the very same issue months prior. I will also tell of that later in detail. It amazes me how protective people are over molesters. Is it not wrong?

For many years, I held the responsibility of being touched inappropriately, taking complete ownership of my wrong doing, reaching out to a God that my mother once knew, hoping that He could hear my request for help. I really hoped that He could hear me. I desperately needed Him to hear me. I had nowhere else to turn. I wished that He would keep me from making these decisions to ask a grown man to distort my innocence. I really needed Him to allow me to recognize or even consider the moment I asked, because I could not remember asking to be put in a situation that scared me to death.

I thought that maybe I had blanked out during this moment. I could vaguely remember being one who daydreamed a great deal. My attention span was so short that I could never complete a task, but started many before the day's end. I have actually mastered the skill of finishing everything I start. Now it is called multitasking. It's funny how my inconsistency became a viable skill. People talked about me so much I started working hard at trying to fix things that others told me were wrong, becoming my own worst critic. I pushed myself to OCD at one point.

That was very unhealthy. I still battling certain aspects of that and the Army didn't make it any better.

(Laughing) I used to think that I would never be able to drive. I did not think that I would be able to pay attention to the road long enough to keep safe. My mind drifted excessively often, unreasonably often. Maybe it was in these moments that I invited the predators to take advantage of me without realizing what I was asking for.

God never responded. Maybe He was mad at me for my mother's choice to leave His town. Maybe we were too far away for Him to hear me. Seemed as if the more I prayed the worse life would get for me. Did my mom now work for the devil? What in the hell was happening?

Now my mother was unwavering about us girls not being in the faces of men and by no means were we ever to sit in a man's lap, but she never told me what to do if a man came into my bed or invaded my personal space. In fact, she had left my cousin to baby-sit. I guess when I think about it, we had been alone so often, it wouldn't have mattered if he was there or not.

As an adult, I have come to know that I have completely no control over the actions of anyone but myself and at times even that thought was sketchy. These men were just bad men who made bad choices. The women who did nothing about it, or accused me of provoking these men were just as disturbed.

I've often questioned the possibility of ignorance. How can an unlearned person be held responsible for their actions? If no one has ever chastised them or have ever pointed out the fact that their actions were unacceptable, are they ever held accountable?

I question the root of their acts and begin to wonder where this behavior was learned to begin with.

Was this something that had been done to them, or was it embedded within their nature? Then I question, if this is something that is in their nature, then they would also have to possess the idea or thought of doing the right thing. This then trumps the whole ignorance alibi and creates the reality of choice. They are the center of what is right and wrong, and possess both within them. Right and wrong are one, housed in one body, until divided by choice. Now my wheels are spinning... Choice, hmm!

NOT ALL MISERY LOVES COMPANY

As time progressed and nothing else, my eldest sister was murdered, I was taken into the foster care system, now separated not only from God, but my mother. I was moved from one person's home to the next in a very short span of time, facing challenges in each home. The one home that I remember the most would allow me to draw closer to God. I felt it. (I have always used my sister's death as an excuse for why we were taken away from my mother, but the truth is, it was my fault, my sister didn't die until after we were in the foster care system. I have held this secret for years, but I will explain it in a different chapter.)

I had encountered several girls in the foster home who shared their stories with me. Stories that made my situation seem as if God had been there all the while.

When I heard tell of a girl my age, ten at the time having sex with her father and her mother allowing it, it made being touched inappropriately appear harmless. The idea of a mother allowing it was crazy to me. My mother wasn't the greatest, but she wouldn't allow anyone to say boo too loud to me in her presence, without going off on him or her.

This led me to believe that God had stopped these men from doing any real harm to me, regardless of their choice. I felt that maybe He did hear me after all.

During bedtime, my roommate and I would converse about all sorts of things. (Laughing) I thought I was a transformer. I would tell her that during certain hours of the night my body would be taken over by my transformer. I promised her that she could come and be one also, if she could stay awake long enough. She would always fall to sleep. I used that as my justification for why she missed all the fun and would give her a graphic detail of the mission I had accomplished without her.

My brother and I use to make believe we were transformers when I was still at home with mom. It was all that I had left of him after we had been separated, or at least the best memory. I was still playing transformers, had imaginary friends, and was dreaming of the year 2000, I just knew cars would fly and we would live like the JETSONS.

My roommate had very different thoughts of what fun was. She thought fun was having sex with her father and she missed it. Now I can't quite remember if she actually thought it was fun, but I remember her saying that she missed it. She thought that it was normal and asked if my father did that to me. Although I had been molested, I had never had intercourse and I was unwilling to share that information with her. I thought it was wrong for us to talk this way. Besides, I didn't want to believe those things happened to me. I would much rather believe I was a transformer and there was more than meets the eye.

I was so damned confused, because in that assembly, it was stated that no adult, man, or woman was supposed to touch you inappropriately, ever! While I was perturbed by being touched by a man, she explained that her father was putting his penis inside of her vagina. I was horrified. I really did not need to know this. God had truly been there all along. He stopped this from happening to me. I was still a virgin. She was not and could never get that gift back.

Now at the time, I thought molestation was sex, I was clueless of intercourse because I had never experienced it. She would explain that she had been placed in the Foster Home because her mother finally called the police on her father.

She told me that they lived in a hotel. Her father, mother, and two siblings shared a room with two beds. She said that her father would send her mom and siblings to the store and would make her stay. During this time he would perform sexual acts on her, telling her to pretend his penis was like candy and had her to suck on him while reciting certain phrases. This sh*t[2] was sick.

I shed tears for the girls who were experiencing the unimaginable and began to ask God to send His angels to protect them. They needed the angels more than I did. I had to become stronger to protect myself. Promising not to be selfish and only ask God for help when it was necessary. I did not want God to help me when there were

---

[2] My apologies for the profanity, I use these words not for lack of a better term, but because it is the one word that best described my feeling at this moment. I will try to keep it at a minimum when possible

so many others with a greater need. I began to feel guilty any time I would ask God for the simplest of things. Things like peace of mind, or even a stable home. I felt it was selfish of me to want too much comfort when people were being violated by their own fathers.

LOL...
CHURCH!
CHAPTER 2

I MAY HAVE MISTAKEN EMOTION FOR THE SPIRIT OF GOD.

As destiny would have it, my great grandmother moved in to the town that my mother had relocated us to, in efforts to obtain custody of me. Another prayer answered. This may have been the first lesson I learned about God's timing as opposed to my own. It was at this moment that I understood that old phrase "God may not come when you want Him to, but He is always right on time."

Was this a manifestation of my own Will, coincidence or the works of God?

I moved with my great grandmother and life began to feel so balanced, stable to say the least, for a while.

She loved me. She loved me. She loved me. I felt it. I have always felt her love.

It was unlike any other love I have felt. The love that only a mother can extend to the child she has given birth to herself. It is funny that as much as I loved and adored my own mother, I have never received that type of love from her in return after her drastic transition into a new character.

Though still apart from my mother, which was my only real concern, I was doing well. This whole situation could be considered coincidence, irony, or just purpose. I will allow you to be the judge.

I had to be about eleven years of age at this time, just entering the sixth grade. Having missed so much school, I still managed to score the highest amongst the top three students in my school on the proficiency exams administered to the entire student body.

Presently, most things seem like second nature to me, as if they were understood prior to me being introduced to them. All things seem to me as if I am remembering things that I have already been exposed to prior to present moments. Things are always familiar to me, always have been. Individuals have always stated that I am good at everything, but it is not that I am good at them, things just make sense, as if I've done it before.

Speaking of second nature, my great grandmother took me to the second hand store to purchase dresses for me so that I might attend church. This brings me back to how my first memory of church was with her. Now my first memory of being reintroduced to church is with her. Coincidence?

My eldest sister was murdered in early December, so my reflection of this night at church being New Year's

Eve is relatively precise. It all seemed like the same month, but I am almost certain a year or so had passed.

I still hold some scattered memories of things that I cannot completely recall, or maybe I choose not to.

I can remember a woman on the pulpit preaching. She preached about how we go day by day struggling and not asking God for our needs. She explained how God's Word was a contract and we needed to remind God of the terms. She explained that when we felt that our prayers were not being answered we needed to familiarize ourselves with the contract. It was the only way to know what we are entitled to have.

I remember the people in the church jumping and shouting just as I had done when I was a child. I watched tears flow from the eyes of adult men, whom I had thought were not supposed to cry. I watched my great grandmother thank God for the safe return of her baby, which I am assuming she meant me. I was overwhelmed and wanted to release all of the bubbles that were trapped under my skin. I wanted to cry and shout. My heart felt like it was going to burst. I was losing control. I was literally feeling what these people were responding to. I struggled immensely to maintain control of myself. I was not what these people were. Surely they were members of something that I was only invited to partake in.

As the New Year drew closer, the intensity of praise grew stronger. The magnitude of the worship was trance like. The bellowing of these people became more and more intense. It was powerful whatever it was. I could not hold my tears back by the time of alter call. I felt my soul cry out. I had lost control. I believe I had been formally introduced to God or the spirit thereof. As I looked around, I was fearful of anyone knowing that I was feeling this way without paying or signing up for it.

"Is there one?" the man called. "Is there one who will give there life back to God, is there one?"

Wow, he was talking to me!

I looked around, and was the only one not engaged in worship, outside of a few crying babies who were being ignored, and a few little boys who were playing with toy cars, engaged as if they were oblivious to anything going on around them. I had to assume that these happenings would leave an impression in the mental makeup of these children that would affect the direction of their lives and choices indefinitely, as it has certainly done to me.

He had to be talking to me.

"Is there one who will repent for the remission of their sins and be baptized in the name of Jesus'?"

Yep, he was talking to me, but what sin? I still didn't know what I had done so wrong. It was later explained to me that we are all born in sin. Therefore, I was repenting for my sinful creation. The fact that I was born with the ability to do wrong was a sin in itself.

I am laughing now because something never really sat right with me concerning that theory or philosophy. I couldn't make any sense of it at all. It did not make sense then, and it does not make sense now in the manner in which it had been taught. Why should I apologize for being who I am? I felt like the person who made me should hold all of the responsibility not me. However, who was I to point out to grown people how stupid they sound? I figured it wasn't that simple if they didn't get it.

Who in their right mind, having a choice would subject themselves to serving a god who considered them guilty before innocent, when he made them that way? It sounds like a bunch of bullsh*t to me. Either some intellectual is misrepresenting God, or this is not the right god.

Through later studies, I have understood clearly the intent behind those teachings and have learned that God is not the accuser, god is. I will help you later to understand my thought process behind the manner in which I speak so candidly. The chapter called "God or god?" will explain it.

My mother told me that there was power in that name Jesus. That very name is what caused me to stand up and walk to that man. Not so much the name, but the power associated with the name.

I told that man that I was the one. I was the one to be baptized in the name of Jesus. Felt as if he knew it was someone that was supposed to come to him and he had not a clue, all at the same time. I knew it was I and wouldn't budge until I felt some type of reassurance, some security in knowing that my decision was not self- motivated. I needed to know that this was not just emotion, but also some type of supernatural pull similar to gravity.

I wouldn't budge, of course until I heard that name Jesus. I believed that the power in that name was what gave me the courage to walk to the front of that church. Otherwise, it would have never happened. I was not only shy, but also insecure. Now that I think about it, without the name, I kind of felt like I was being initiated in some type of cult, like I had walked into some type of ritual, where all the people had invoked spirits that were causing them to behave in a peculiar manner. They were speaking in tongues[3], which could be misconstrued as chanting, but the fact is, I wholeheartedly believe in speaking in tongues and the Holy Ghost.

---

[3] Acts 2:4 - And they were all filled with the Holy Ghost, and began to speak with other tongues, as the Spirit gave them utterance. The bible would explain that the speaking in tongues is the evidence of having received the gift of the Holy Ghost.

The Holy Ghost…it just sounds funny, I am sorry! I do believe that the "Holy Ghost" is the spirit of God, the same spirit that was said to have descended upon Christ in the form of a dove. If Christ is our example, one would have to assume that the same would occur for us. While the bible explains that it is a gift that "Shall" be received after repentance, then all who have repented "Shall" receive it. I do not believe that everyone has spoken in tongues or has to, to have received the "Holy Ghost". I believe that speaking in tongues is the language in which the spirit within us utilizes to communicate with the higher power on the behalf of this physical being which merely houses our spirit. I could very well be wrong, but thank God for personal faith. It works for me.

That night also happened to be a communion night and they kept talking about drinking Jesus' blood and eating his flesh to remember Him. There was a white cloth covering what looked like a body lying across an alter that read "In Remembrance of Me". It was somewhat frightening to tell you the total truth. Somehow, something was still drawing me to it. Thinking back, I am sure it was the music playing that contributed to me being drawn in. Like hypnosis! That shout music will get you every time. It's like soul food with a twang.

When I read what I just wrote, the things that I have grown up with all my life sound like a cult or some type of African tribal ritual. Now don't get me wrong, I am not knocking anyone's faith or belief, I am just simply pointing out that these things are very similar to the very exact things that I have been taught against. These things were parallel to the average cult. Am I the only one that recognizes it? An altar, a chalice, blood, human flesh, a cross, candles, music, men and woman in robes, invocation of a spirit, chanting in an unfamiliar tongue, praying for power, baptisms symbolic of a watery grave, being reborn unto new life, I mean come on, you have to admit! I know church people, excuse me, I mean people who attend church would call what I am saying blasphemy. I am really just stating the obvious. I mean no harm. I still do and believe some of the very same things.

It just so happens that every time I decide to go to church, it turns out to be communion Sunday. I always partake in communion after careful examination of myself. I remember growing up, communion felt like walking the Green Mile. Just image a 3 day consecration[4] and fasting, with no water, no food no television and being shut in the church with the rest of the congregation. Could you imagine, as a child, hearing the cries and lamentations of people who were desperately seeking forgiveness for all of the sin that they have committed throughout the year, urgently fixing the problem prior to entering the New Year. We were constantly forewarned by

---

[4] Consecration was to produce the ritual transformation of our bodies, rendering ourselves hallow and worthy of the ingestion of body and blood of Jesus. We were setting ourselves apart from the world in preparation for communion.

the pastor of the woes of God's wrath upon us. We were reminded that we would burn eternally with hell fire and brimstone. We were reminded of the gnashing of the teeth of individuals who were already dead and who did not clear themselves of their sins prior to their passing away. They were said to have been given an indestructible body that would burn forever and ever. I was told that I had better pray and that Jesus was coming soon. I needed to prepare myself for the inevitable, because the pastor constantly repeated, "You're damned if you do, and you are damned if you don't". I was scared sh*tless y'all. This meant that no matter what, I was going to hell, because regardless of how much I prayed and repented, I was still born in sin and I would die in sin. My only question would become, what then was the purpose of Christ?

Moving forward, I was baptized that New Year's day at exactly twelve mid-night. While offering my life to God as a living sacrifice, I could only think of my mother's praise. I tell of this situation to offer greater example of things that seem to be divinely purposed. How profound is it that I was with my great grandmother when I gave my life to God, and it was New Years, the one day out of the year that my mother faithfully dedicated to God after becoming what religion calls a backslider.

AND THE MORNING AND EVENING WERE THE FIRST DAY

My great grandmother was tripping. She told me now that I was saved, I had to give up all of my pants, and no earrings or make up. What the hell? I didn't wear earrings or makeup so that was no problem, but my pants?

First of all, I never asked to be saved, I didn't even know what I was being saved from. I was doing fine with my pants thank you very much. How can you take pants from a tomboy? I DID NOT sign up for this. No one told me I could not wear pants if I was "saved", before I was saved? Truthfully, my decision to be baptized would have been calculated appropriately.

As sad as it may sound, I was rethinking this whole saved thing. I thought that maybe I responded in haste upon the onset of emotions during that church service. Man, what the hell did I get myself into? I demand a do over.

It was too late. At this point the choice was no longer my own, this lifestyle eventually became a burden to me. I felt so trapped, even more so because I would never disobey my great grandmother. Therefore, that meant I was stuck living a lie. There were times when I was submissive to God because I loved him and really wanted a relationship with Him, but not at the expense of my happiness. Had I not suffered enough? This was just uncalled for.

There were other times when I could not be submissive because I resented the church and church people. Everyone including myself seemed so hypocritical.

I just flat out got tired of faking and would not do it any longer.

Because I was forced to go to church and did not respond to the move of the "spirit", I was a silent outcast within the church. They could not totally disown me because I was still in attendance.

My great grandmother was pretty good at making an effort to explain things to me and teaching me about God, but I was still feeling forced into a lifestyle that brought me great discomfort. I mean, no offense to God or anyone's beliefs, but I really didn't want to serve a god who was concerned about what I was wearing if my heart was right. I could have been the worse b*tch ever, but as long as my dress was to my ankles and I gave an appearance of being saved, these folks put me in heaven. I could have faked my tongues and drank a bottle of wine at twelve years of age "In Remembrance of Him" and it would have been totally justified. I would call it delinquency of a minor.

When I am wrong, tell me I am wrong, and by all means, please help me fix me. Don't just condemn me. I do that enough on my own. I am truly my own worst critic. That's how I was feeling. Trapped

I know I was a child, but it did not take a warhead technologist to see that something was not right. There were people in this church who were revered at a very high esteem within the congregation. These people were in clicks. They loved my great grandmother, but hated me for no apparent reason. They gossiped instead of helping others, they were just plain old nasty. Yet I still tried everything to fit in for a while, to no avail. I guess I was just as bad for judging them.

I was always the underdog, who hung out with the underdogs. These saved people were cruel. One minute lying on you and mistreating you, the next praising God. They would bless God with the very same tongue they had just cursed me with. I still don't know what I did to deserve it, or why I didn't stand up for myself back then. I will honestly say that not all church folk are bad folk. There are some righteous hearted people with a genuine care, who are in search of true righteousness. These were the individuals who kept me holding on to the bit of faith that I had left. There had to be some positives to this lifestyle, or there would not be so many people converting. I held on for dear life to this hope. It would become my saving grace.

Sporadically within the congregation, there would be that one old woman who admired me. She would always acknowledge me and offer me an undefined kindness, kindness irregular in nature, sort of melancholy.

One would almost swear that the presence of God could be felt in her touch. I would get the feeling that she almost felt sorry for me, knowing something about me that I did not understand about myself, but proud nonetheless. It was a constant reminder of the elder who touch my hand as a younger child.

My great grandmother loved me, maybe one of the very few in life who actually did, and unconditionally. She would always tell me that I was special and that God was going to use me. I still cry for her at times. I often have a memory of biting beads off a white comforter on her bed. I eventually found that memory to be very real. I will tell of that later, maybe in this book, or maybe in the next, however God sees fit. I do not know why telling you that is relevant, but hey, there you have it! It seemed fitting at first, then I read it and now I cannot figure out what it has to do with the price of tea in China. Don't judge me! (laughing)

AND YE SHALL SURELY DIE

CHAPTER 3

SHE WOULD STILL BE ALIVE HAD YOU TOLD SOMEONE

We relocated once again and my grandmother moved us into her daughter's home. She was my mother's aunt, my great aunt. I can recall my mother stating that this aunt had been her trial[5]. I was to understand why at a later time. She also became my trial.

For the sake of not having to constantly write "great grandmother", I will use the name Mamita. That is what we called her. It is Spanish for mother.

Mamita died shortly after we moved in with my aunt. I was to be blamed for her death by my aunt. Well, I call it blame, but again, you are the judge. I am more than sure if asked, she would call me a liar, as she always did.

---

[5] The type of trial I speak of is the state of pain or anguish that tests patience, endurance, or a person's belief

I am also sure she cannot come up with any true accounts of me misbehaving as she would tell it.

The day my grandmother died, my aunt asked me to state the series of events that had taken place prior to her passing. I did just that. In listening to the things that I told her, her cold harsh response was "If you would have told someone, mamma would still be alive."

I would take on the responsibility of Mamita's death and seize that very blame for most of my teenage years before receiving any closure, that closure came just weeks ago after talking to my first cousin. She explained that Mamita chose to confide in me above all others. All others saw it as if she had confided in a child. They may not have liked the fact that she trusted me.

Thanks cousin. That was truly a comfort to my soul.

That day, Mamita was searching for her car keys. She was going to pick up my other aunt and cousins for our church service that evening. She requested that everyone help her find her keys. My cousins were too caught into their video game to assist. This upset her. I fearfully watched as she grabbed her chest in anguish. It was no surprise because she had done this several times in the past several weeks.

My cousins were totally innocent in the matter. They were children and just really wanted to play. I am more than sure that we all would have responded a little differently had we understood the situation for what it was worth.

She had actually changed drastically over those last weeks. I notice that she was putting salt in her food and butter on her toast. This was strange because I never saw that. She even started using real sugar in her coffee as oppose to the supplemental sweeteners that she swore by.

We finally found the keys and proceeded to my auntie's house. I was always so excited to go there because of my younger cousins. I had always been so fond of them. It seemed as if they were the only family members that at the time, that were pleased to have me around. I always felt welcomed without feeling a sense of being responsible for my mother's decisions. Which is how I assume the adults in the family viewed me. If nothing more, it's how they made me feel.

Mamita pulled over on the side of the road twice before reaching our destination. I asked her if she was feeling alright. She continued to hold her chest as if the pain she felt was unbearable. It was painful for me to watch because I could not do anything to help.

"I am ok baby" was her reliable response.

Although I did not believe her, I accepted her word and continued to keep watch over her as well as pray. I had no clue of what I was praying about, I just wanted her pain to go away.

I cannot recall much about that night's service, but I remember my aunt asking if I wanted to stay for midnight prayer. During this stage in my life, I did not know how to say no, even if yes meant my discomfort and unhappiness. The reality was I wanted to be with Mamita, not midnight prayer.

Mamita realized that I did not want to stay and told me that I did not have to stay if I did not want to. So I was happy to head home.

We made it home that night, but not into the house until a few hours later. Mamita, with her head lying across the steering wheel, in a unresponsive manner, sustained a whimper of inescapable agony. I begged her to allow me to seek help, I begged God for help. Please God, help me...

I was never a disobedient child and would never disrespect her, so I accepted her order not to tell anyone of her illness. I did not know then that her will to live had expired.

We eventually made it into the main house, and headed toward the attached apartment where we were residing. On the way, I passed my uncle as he was watching television in his bedroom. I paused for a brief moment, contemplating on whether or not I should be disrespectful and not honor her wishes. I just wanted to get her some help. In all honesty, I never once considered the possibility of her dying. It never crossed my mind.

I began to recall the times prior to this night, when she sat with me, giving me an order of service for what appeared to be a funeral and obituary. She would explain what songs she wanted sang, the color of her casket and several other requests in the case of her death. She directed me to the whereabouts of her important documents and any other items she deemed necessary for me to know. I did not realize it then, but she had an exact knowledge of her passing away and prepared me for it as if it was normal. She was ready and willing to return unto the God that gave her.

That night I did not sleep at all. Every time I would hear her cry, I would jump to her rescue, bringing her water and laying my head on her shoulder in an attempt to comfort her. I prayed harder that night than I could ever remember praying.

I demanded one last time, "Mamita please let me go and get Auntie!"

"No baby, don't go get your aunt, I will be alright."

After those last words, I heard the most piercing sound proceed from her soul. The sound stifled my heartbeat and vexed my spirit. I made the toughest decision that I thought I would ever have to make.

I disobeyed her wishes, and hasten down the stair. I told my aunt that there was something wrong with Mamita.

"No baby, don't go get your aunt, I will be alright." These were her last words. She died that afternoon.

I still sometimes wish I had told someone that she was ill. I understood afterwards, that it might have saved her life. I also know that those thoughts were selfish ones. I was not sad that she died, she prepared me for that. I was sad for myself, because I no longer had her to love me and protect me from the perils that I was scheduled to face.

I feel now as an adult that my great grandmother strategically placed me in my aunt's home, trusting that I would be safe in that environment, or if nothing else, I would be raised in the church.

Her calculations were accurate. I was raised in the church. I won't go into many details about my home life now, but I will say that it was a living hell wrapped in a lavish array of this is bullsh*t.

I had luxuries and comfort but was abused sexually, physically, verbally and emotionally. I was broken down at every angle. I was never allowed to be human and make a mistake. Even my good was discredited. I was called a liar constantly and challenged as if I were an adult. I lived every moment of my teenage years concerned. I was living day by day with knots in my belly, constantly praying that I did nothing wrong that day for fear of being slapped in my face or having my hair pulled and slung around like a rag doll. What amazes me even more is that adults stood around and watched as if it were normal, as if I had done something worthy of that type of punishment. No one stepped in.

I would dare not tell my mother of the things that were happening. She had already lost her eldest child. I could not burden her with this minor stuff. Even if... what would she do about it? Did she care? She had never attempted to get my sisters and I back.

I understand now, that she felt as if we would be better off without her. She had blamed herself for my eldest sister's death. She did not want to be the cause of my destruction.

MY TRIAL AND SOME TRIBULATIONS BEGAN

I was a virgin, an honor roll student and an awesome big sister, if I must say so myself. I am sure my sisters will tell a very different tale. Our views of life are not the same. In my mind, I had taken care of my two younger siblings as if I gave birth to them myself.

Even that was challenged by my aunt; it was thought that I had too much control. She drew a wedge between my sisters that would last a life time.

It really was not that I had too much control. I just had to protect them. I was the eldest. Even if that meant I had to sacrifice me. Sacrifice…

When Mamita died, I died with her. I died each day, choosing to be who the hell I wanted to be, until I got home from school. Then my aunt's reality set in.

School was my outlet. I begin to strive for a form of excellence. I was able to create my own reality of who I was without disclosing my dysfunctional home life.

We lived in a large two story home and I rode to school in a Mercedes Benz. It was easy to convince folk that I had it good. Besides, my aunt always stressed that what happened in our house stayed in our house. That remained true until she would get on the pulpit and preach an exaggerated story about my life.

Who does that? (Laughing) and these damned church members would shout as if she was preaching the gospel. She was the essence of a gossip preacher. And would have the nerve to ask me how she did. I would lie as usual, "You were great aunty." I don't understand why she ever believed that lie when she accused me of lying about everything true.

They say preachers kids are the worse. They are. Take a closer look at their parents and the proof is always there.

That is not always true, but I am speaking for the ones that I have encountered personally.

Honestly though, I could appreciate my aunt's style of preaching, she couldn't sing worth a damn, but the presence of confidence that would shine around her, I admired so much. She was poised, one of the very same characteristics that I have inherited. For some odd reason, I was always seeking her approval.

The truth was I hated when she would preach about me. It would have been different if the things were true and she helped me to fix all that was wrong.

I could not understand how people could be in church so long, reading the bible every day and miss the message. It always made me question their motive.

At 16years old, I had my first conversation with God.

ADAM, WHERE ARE YOU?

CHAPTER 4

WHERE WAS I?

I sat in Sunday school not listening to a word my aunt was teaching. I sat silently questioning where I was. I knew where I was, in the physical sense, but where was I? Why was I?

I remembered reading in the King James Version of the bible, the book of Genesis where God asked Adam where he was[6]. I can bluntly conclude that those who had taught me this story in times past had not considered this, but I could not help but think about what God asked. "Adam, where are you?"

Now this doesn't make sense to me. Why would God, the ALMIGHTY, ask where Adam was if He knows all things?

---

[6] Genesis 3:9 And the Lord God called unto Adam, and said unto him, Where art thou

Was I to discredit God? Certainly not, but I was to diligently seek an understanding of God's intent.

I concluded that God asked that question because He wanted Adam to recognize where he was. Not in the physical sense, but where was he spiritually?

He had been separated from God. With the receiving of knowledge of good and evil, came the distancing of true communication with God, the separation from partaking in his God like nature. Adam was dead.

I have always come to know death as being physically removed from life, as we know it, to no longer exist. On the contrary, to die[7] has also been defined as to long keenly. Adam surely did not die in the sense that he no longer existed, but he longed keenly to commune with God, for he had not an understanding of the knowledge that he obtained. To know and understand are very different. I know a whole lot of things that I do not understand.

Like Adam, I once had a relationship with God unbeknown to me. I was Naked and living freely without condemnation. When I made a choice to be "saved", so to speak, and obtain all of the knowledge of God that the

> And he said, I heard thy voice in the garden, and I was afraid, because I was naked; and I hid myself.
>
> And he said, who told thee that thou wast **Naked**?

---

[7] Die: To experience an agony or suffering suggestive of that of death

church offered, I began to possess a certain level of antipathy towards God. I began distancing myself, searching, longing for my truth. I surely died, covering my shame as I went. I begin to view this God differently than I ever had before. I had concluded that this was not the God that I wanted to serve. I felt that I have chosen a path that imprisoned me as well as my spiritual growth, because of the inconsistency of the teaching and the inability of the ministers to counter my inquiry, without calling me a devil for being curious.

If the Tree of Knowledge of Good and Evil was forbidden, why do we come to church to be taught knowledge of good and evil? If the Tree of life was to be eaten from freely, why don't we just live?

"We are not to question God" was the infamous answer. That's the wrong damn answer!

The bible specifically tells us to seek[8] and we shall find, ask and we shall receive, it also says that if we knock, the doors will be opened for us. So quite naturally, in order to receive an answer you have to ask the question.

I knew that something had to give, but what? Where was I?

As did Adam, I chose to accept what was pleasant to my eyes even after questioning myself about the validity of what was taking place in this religion that night I was baptized. My intentions were meant for the good, and I honestly believed that at 12, I was responsible enough to make that decision.

As God asked Adam, I feel that I was also being questioned by God…Gina where are you?

---

[8] Matthew 7:7-8 Ask, and it shall be given you; seek, and ye shall find; knock, and it shall be opened unto you: For every one that asketh receiveth; and he that seeketh findeth; and to him that knocketh it shall be opened.

My answer would be, "I am hiding Lord because I am Naked." He would then ask, "Who told you that you were Naked?" I would simply respond, "The Church"

I do so genuinely believe in God, a supreme being, the ineffable[9], but this was not my idea of whom or what God represented. That day I explained to God that I was really trying to live a saved life, but I did not understand why I could never obtain the perfection that the church so desperately sought from me. I was going in a constant circle for nothing, if Christ had already died for my sins.

What good was Christ if I had to put him back on the cross every time I did something wrong? This notion was consistent with the Law of Moses who gave atonement for sin yearly through sacrificial offerings. But if Christ was the sacrifice, for once and for all, then the

---

[9] Ineffable: Incapable of being expressed; indescribable or unutterable.

Law of Moses has been fulfilled and is inadequate in comparison to the death and resurrection of Christ. So why was I being forced to live according to a law that has been fulfilled. Was Christ not the sacrifice that did away with all sin? If so, why did I not feel saved at church? I felt more saved when I was merely being myself, by myself. Before righteousness was a requirement, it was easy.

I will explain what I mean in terms that make more sense. Let's say you have a student loan that will take you a lifetime to pay off. This loan is a serious burden and it is constantly getting in the way of your progression in life. You come to me with the burden and I pay it all, every dime. Once it is all paid for and I give you the letter of satisfaction, why would you continue to make monthly payments for something that has already been paid for? Doesn't make much sense does it? Well, this is how I was feeling about the church's rule by the Law of Moses. The Law is inadequate when placed before the Law of Christ, which is to love your neighbor as you love yourself. I don't think this is much to ask for after being crucified and resurrected for us. If I love you, naturally, I will not kill you, steal from you, and covet your husband or wife, or any of the other things listed in the Commandments. I think the problem of this world are two very significant things, one we do not know the word of God for ourselves and two, we simply do not love ourselves. So we treat others the way we feel about ourselves. Love truly conquers all; it sums up the Commandments in a nutshell. The simplicity of the gospel amazes me. I never got why man makes it more difficult than it truly is. I digress.

I explained to God that I was not willing to pretend to be what they wanted me to be. I had a good heart and felt that I had done nothing wrong, other than what the church dubbed sin. And those things I had not a problem with.

The things I regarded as sin, I did not partake in. It was all the other rules that I just did not believe that God cared about, the things that were mandated by the church, but I could not find anywhere in the bible, and believe me, I searched. I searched when I would get into trouble. My punishment was to write books of the bible, word for word. It was never really a punishment, but a blessing in disguise.

In fact, the bible read the exact opposite of what I was being taught, minus some truths. I felt that the church made living for God an unnecessarily impossible chore. I was damned if I did, and damned if I didn't, so why not?

I was subject to punishment and judgment when the time of judgment had not come yet. I was a child, how could anyone put me in hell when they had no clue of who I was to become in my future? They did not know what "God" had planned for me and neither did I.

They were succeeding in pushing me further and further away from Him. That doesn't sound like the works of God to me. However, what if it was?

What if God was asking where I was, for me to realize the state I was in? Maybe my call was not what I thought it was.

I told God that I did not think it was fair that these grown people forced me to be saved, when the choice is supposed to be my own. I did not think it was fair that they had an opportunity to live their lives first, before making a decision to commit to this sort of lifestyle. I was so uncomfortable with being forced to live a certain way and be fatefully judge when I never asked to be here.

How was I to know if this lifestyle was right for me when I was always so unhappy? I was limited to everything that would cause me joy. I wanted to be free.

I was a virgin, I didn't drink, and well....It was communion I tell ya! That's my story and I am sticking to it. (Laughing) But I was a good girl. My grades were good and I was respectful, what else did they want from me?

I just wanted to hang out and be normal. They said that I was not like the world. What does that even mean? I was raised to think I was better than everyone who did not go to our church, or anyone who was not a part of our denomination. That was just flat out wrong. It eliminated me from talking to more than half my family. How could I be a witness to the world if I kept my nose up at them?

I remember when my two cousins got pregnant at an early age, I was told not to hold their babies, as if they had some type of disease. This is crazy. Where am I?

To God, I acknowledged Him as being God. I explained that I would surely come back to Him if He would allow me to just live my life, taking into consideration that He is worthy of praise, regardless of me.

From that moment on, life for me began to take many twists and turns, turns that would instigate the evolution of my spiritual travel to seek knowledge and its understanding. I would ultimately challenge the idea of *love, life, religion* and *God*. I was on a uniquely designed quest to find a real God, the real God.

THE SHORT, OF THE LONG OF IT

CHAPTER 5

STONE COLD

We moved around quite a bit, sh*t, a whole lot... way too much for any one person, especially a child. Now it was not like being in the military, where the moves are beneficial. These moves were evictions and living with strange people, who were called cousin so and so.

I will not use names, and if I do, the names will be changed to protect the truth about folks, because people have a tendency to avoid truth at all cost. I will even go so far as to say that these are my truths alone, my way of seeing things, nevertheless the truth. And it hurts.

However, it is my life and I needed to face my realities in order to free myself from me. I will explain that later also.

My mother introduced us to so many men that I can't count them. That is a bit exaggerated, but there were a lot. A few stuck out amongst others.

Bird was one of my favorites. He was really nice to us and he had a laugh like goofy. I wish I could spell his laugh for you, but I don't think you would get the true essence of the humor. I use to try to tell jokes just to hear him laugh. That is really all I remember about him, other than seeing him from time to time throughout my life span while with my mother.

Then there was Luther. He would become the father of one of my mother's children. He came around every now and again, but not much. When asked where he was, the response was either, "at the Log" or "in jail." It was always an ongoing joke. My mother found it hilarious that those places are where my sister would assume her father was at any given time.

Jail is self-explanatory, but the "Log" was a hangout for individuals who lived in the small town. It was in the alley behind a small community store, where I would always purchase chocolate NOW AND LATERS, they were $0.10 for a six-piece package. $0.50 was like payday for me. Old a** drunk men, who would hang out with my mom and grandmother, would give me nickels and dimes just for being cute. Or because they thought, my mother and grandmother were cute and only treated me nice for Brownie point. I would also get nickels and dimes because I would tell them about how well I did on my report card. That was always a good dollar after collecting from each old man. Especially, one man in particular, my grandmother's boyfriend Nate.

Stone!

I just call that "N" word Stone Cold. Please excuse my language, but again, I use certain terms, not for the lack of a better word, but that word best describes what I am intending to put into words. I hate the "N" word. But I don't know how else to describe Stone to you.

He was every bit of the word "nigga," my definition at least. He was a worthless piece of weak a** black man. Every negative stereotype that was created to describe black people is exactly what he was. And that is being nice.

I had always thought that when blacks were captured and brought to America, only the strongest were selected. Boy was I wrong. Stone's a** must have slipped through the damn cracks. I guess you have noticed by now, that I did not like Stone very much.

He was insecure; freakin' weak and uncivilized is how I describe any man who beats on a woman who cannot defend herself against him. Why not pick fights with a man?

He used to beat my mother's a**. I hated him. I hated him even more when I ran into him as an adult. I ran into him in a laundry mat, he was with some woman. I could not help but think that he was probably beating her too, as I rolled my eyes at him as if it were only yesterday that he beat my mom. As much as I would like to excuse him, there is no excuse for him.

One morning I was getting up for school and there was a woman lying on my mother's couch. (No one ever made me go to school. I just really wanted to learn. I was good at it. Reading made me happy and I loved to write even more.) I did not recognize the woman at all. I figured it was one of my mother's friends who may have just stayed the night. As usual, my mother wasn't home and I was late for school. I went into my sister's bedroom to see if she could do something to my hair. She kept telling me to ask mom.

Frustrated, I yelled, trying to explain that mom wasn't home and I was late. I needed my hair combed. As we were yelling back and forth, I heard my mother's voice scream out to us, demanding that we were quiet. She was trying to get some rest.

What the hell? That voice was coming from the couch where that woman was asleep. I went back into the living room to take a closer look. As I got closer, she said again, "quiet the noise, I need to rest."

Jesus Christ! It was my mother lying there, beaten beyond recognition. I ran to my sister's room as quickly as I could and told her that Stone had beaten mom again.

Now my sister was no joke. Although she was a child, she was well respected and feared by most adults I knew. She had been well known around the small town that we lived in called Oak Park, and was known to "beat a bi***'s a**." She also fought boys. She did not discriminate.

She fought kids, woman, men, and even old people if they rubbed her the wrong way. She was notorious for it. No one would ever believe that this beautiful chocolate young girl was as vicious as she was. She never started any mess, but she would definitely finish it.

She hung out with a group of girls that called themselves Smurf's girls. She would iron letters on her pants that spelled out Smurf's Girls in gang styled writing or what was considered gang styled writing. I know it as calligraphy. She also stitched creases into her pants. Smurf was a well-known gang member. These chicks hung out in a park they called Pebble Beach, when I was lucky, she would allow me to tag along. I adored her. She called me her Bay-Bay. This was way before the popular comedy Be Be's kids.

My sister ran into the living room and yelled out at my mom "What the f**k happened to your face?" As she and my mom were discussing the happenings of the night prior, my sister directed my brother to put a large pot of water on the stove to boil and bring her the aluminum bat that was placed behind the kitchen door.

As she began holding ice wrapped in a towel to my mom's face, she explained that this was the last time that Stone was going put his hands on her. We did not have a phone, so the plan was for my brother to run down the street and call the police from the pay phone at Taco Rico's.

911 emergency was nonexistent at that period of time. There was only the asterisk, and the pound sign that were utilized for emergency dialing.

There was a hammering on the front door before my brother could leave the house. My mom and sister tried to get my brother out the back door, but Stone had pushed his way in before he could get completely out. Stone headed directly for my mom. My sister poured that water on him while I attempted to hit him with the bat. She missed him, but enough touched him to catch his attention. She snatched the bat from me and proceeded to beat him with it. She finally got him out of the house.

The police finally arrived as usual, right after everything had taken place. During this time, there was no such thing as domestic violence and even after seeing my mother's battered face, the police refused to do anything. They did not see the crime occur, so nothing could be done. So pretty much, we had to calculate when we thought Stone would decide to beat my mother again and call the police right before it started so that they could make it right on time to see the fight.

What were we to report? "Please come, he might be getting ready to beat my mother again and we need you here to watch him black her eyes and bust her mouth open this time so you can arrest him?"

They never arrested him. We eventually had to move away. That is really all I have allowed myself to remember about my mother's boyfriends. I managed to stay away from home as much as possible to avoid any contact with men.

FREE SPIRITED

I spent most of my time wandering like a vagabond around town alone or following my brother everywhere he went.

My mother had established credit at several moms and pops stores throughout our small town. I would go in and obtain candy, snacks, and food on her line of credit as I maneuvered my way through the city.

Sometimes I did not return home for a couple of days. I don't even think anyone noticed after a while. My mother also disappeared for days at a time. My big sister was always with the two younger girls.

I would tell the mothers of my friends, that my mom said it was fine for me to spend the night. They couldn't ask my mother because we had no phone at home, nor would they dare turn me away because it was already night by the time I would ask. I personally, won't let my thirteen-year-old walk to the store alone.

During summer time, I would wake up first thing in the morning and head directly to Oak Park Swimming Pool with only my bathing suit on. I didn't wear shoes and never had a towel; we barely ever had clean clothes. I went whole summers without putting shoes on.

From the time the pool opened until the time it closed, I was swimming. That was my bath also. It would clean the caked up dirt that would accumulate on the bottom of my feet after walking the day prior.

The pool would close for an hour each day. Within that hour, the park provided lunch for all the kids. It was brunch for me. I never ate breakfast. I still don't eat breakfast.

Once the pool closed, I began to wander the streets. I had a habit of talking to strangers. I would talk and talk and talk about all the things that were taking place in my household. I would also daydream about how I wanted my life to actually be. I would pretend that life was perfect and nothing negative was going on. It was how I coped. I would take rides from strange people. Cars hit me on several occasions, I fell out of trees, and my feet would bleed often from stepping on glass or scraping my big toe too hard. I never complained or cried about it. It was normal for me.

When I was home, my mom and elder sister wasn't. I would then have to take care of the two youngest children, even if that meant begging and borrowing. I did not steal, it was never an option, and my mother didn't play that. She hated lying and stealing. Those things were just simply not allowed. Everything else was in disarray but she stood fast when it came to morals and values. We were very well mannered children who always used proper etiquette.

I DON'T REMEMBER ASKING FOR THAT

I remember coming home one afternoon. No one was home but my two little sisters and my cousin. I was dog-tired and still barefoot and in my bathing suit. It was extremely hot outside and I opened the window to allow the fresh breeze to blow through, before falling asleep on my mother's bed watching television. There was a folding bed right next to my mother's bed that was designated for my sister's and me to sleep on. My sisters were asleep on that bed.

I was having a bad dream, a nightmare. In this dream, I couldn't breathe. Dark heavy pillows were suffocating me and I felt pressure between my legs, I was in a tree straddling a thick branch. It was painful and the pillows were too heavy for me to push off my face. I felt more and more pressure from the branch between my legs. I had to balance myself with my legs to keep from falling as I try to remove the pillows from my face. I couldn't breathe.

I was still feeling the pressure on my body as I begin to wake up from this dream. I felt hot steamy skin on my face. I attempted to focus and saw what I now know to be a porno playing on the television.

My grown cousin was pushing his penis up and down between my legs and up against my vagina. He had my legs closed very tight, so tight that his penis was pinching the insides of my thighs. I started to cry. When he realized that I was now awake, he jumped off me, and his exact words were, "You asked for it kid." Only I still can't remember when I asked him for it. I looked down and the crotch part of my bathing suit was pulled to the side exposing my privacy.

When he got off of me, I grabbed a blanket and my two little sisters and I locked us in the bathroom.

While safely locked away, I made a pallet with the blanket and laid my sisters on the bathroom floor to sleep while I took a bath, probably the first bath I had in months. It was definitely the first time I felt dirty. I sat for hours in the tub trying to replay in my head, the moment I asked this man to do that to me. I got nothing.

I woke up drowning. I had fallen asleep in the tub and damn near drowned to death. I spent what felt like an hour trying to catch my breath before redressing and cuddling on the bathroom floor with my sisters. We stayed in the bathroom until morning. This was the summer before I was to started third grade.

Keep in mind that all these things were taking place when I was between the ages of five and eleven. God had to have been keeping watch over me, or sent His angels. Maybe it was the angels that my mother had asked God to keep around me. Some would call it coincidence that I hadn't been raped, kidnapped, or even killed.

CRACK KILLS

I never really understood why my mother had changed so drastically until I was exposed to her usage of crack cocaine. It had to be out of hand if she was so bold as to use it in front of us and leave little Gerber baby food jars around where we could find them.

We were in the park late one night. I was excited because my mom was there also. My eldest sister and brother were not around much by this stage in life. It was just us three younger ones. When it started to get too dark, I collected my sisters and went searching for my mom. I asked a few older people if they had any idea of where my mother might have been. They all pointed in the same direction, toward a camper. We were tired and hungry. We were told to sit in the front seat of the camper and wait for my mom to come out from the back. I looked in the rearview mirror and saw my mother smoking on a makeshift crack pipe. She had a baby jar with a broken ink pen sticking out. She was using the ink pen as a straw. As she held the pipe in the air, some other person was lighting it for her. This sh*t didn't smell like cigarettes and it was fogging up the whole camper, as both the front and back were all connected. My sisters and I began to cough. It was too much smoke in there.

My mother was a straight up base head. A crack head, a smoker, or whatever you want to call it. She was it. She had it bad. Nevertheless, I still loved her. This explained the drastic change. I am just glad she never got to the point of stealing.

One day my younger sister set the curtains on fire while my mom and I were asleep. My mom tried to play hero and carry the burning curtain down the hallway, through the living room and out the front door. She received third degree burns up and down her shins.

(Laughing) That was a real crack head move right there, I have to admit. It would have made more sense to put out the fire. Duh!

Now here is how it all started. The day prior, I found my mother's crack pipe and a lighter in the nightstand that was settled between her bed and ours. I had this crazy urge to smoke it as she had done. Therefore, I did, until my younger sister woke up and threatened to tell on me for playing with the fire and the baby food jar. Thank God, there were no drugs in it.

I knew that my sister was also messing with that pipe when no one was looking, and accidentally set the curtains on fire. I dared not tell my mom because I myself would have gotten into trouble. I think we may have gotten a bit of a contact while in that camper. What is so damn crazy is that I knew the smell of crack from anywhere and loved the smell of it, just like I love the smell of gas being pumped into the car. Yeah, I know...cray cray.

NEW JACK ITTY-BITTY CITY

My mother started to allow dope dealers to live in our house, G-ball, Smiley, Flossy, Tee, and Marx. Marx, rest his soul, he died with my sister. He was my sister's boyfriend and we were crazy about him.

They were also gang bangers. This was a very different atmosphere and brought a lot of comfort to our lives as well as discomfort. It unquestionably exposed me to more than I needed to know as a young girl. We had cameras outside of our doors, VRC's, Stereos, excessive amounts of food, new bikes, guns and all types of stuff in our house.

My brother and I would sit around and laugh while G-ball and Smiley had the base heads doing all types of crazy things for a small piece of white stuff. They made them race each other around the corner to see who was the fastest. I have to admit it was pretty hilarious and empowering to have a grown person do whatever you told them to do. We were all kids. G-ball and smiley were only about sixteen and seventeen. My brother was always following them around.

My mother didn't pay much attention to us during these days, she stayed locked up in her room with her friends smoking. She never paid for it because it was her house. I did what I wanted to do. I was raising myself. Every now and again, my big sister made me take a bath and combed my hair. She would hug and kiss on me. She always had a pack of Double mint Gum and would offer a piece. I still love that gum today, because the smell of it is all I have left of her.

One morning the music was blasting and we were hanging out in the back yard. Smiley had his gun sitting on top of the radio while they were back there Crip walking and throwing up gang signs. I was so amused, this was real live entertainment. G-ball accidentally kicked the radio and the gun fell and fired off a shot. The shot hit Smiley under his arm. The bullet could have easily gotten anyone of us, but by the grace of God, we were safe and Smiley's shot was not life threatening.

When the police finally came, they made up a story, telling the cops that rival gang members had shot Smiley in a drive-by. The police bought the story. All the while, I am in shock. I could not believe that I had just watched someone get shot.

My brother was now starting to sell drugs, following the example of our house guests. He would come, give me his gun and drugs, and have me hide them under my mattress. I promised not to let my mom know that I had it, and I didn't. When my brother left the room, I would get the gun and play with it. I had no clue that it was loaded. I looked down the barrel, pointed it toward the room that my mom was in, and all kinds of other crazy things.

Remember, I would fantasize a lot. I probably thought I was John Wayne. However, it was more on the lines of Flossy, Tee's girlfriend. The first and only female dope dealer I had ever met. I wanted to be Flossy. I thought she was so pretty and she dressed nice.

In addition to all of these people selling drugs in our house, my sister's boyfriend Marx did also. He took very good care of my sister. She wore the best of everything. Guess jeans and gold everywhere. She had purchased laser tag for us. It was one of the most high- tech games in the 80's.

Marx was eighteen, she was fifteen, and they were in love. My mom was too caught into her own thing that she didn't realize or care that her daughter was having sex in her house. My sister had already gotten one abortion that my mom knew nothing about.

My mother was dead set against abortions. I know because she once told me that she ran up and down stairs trying to get rid of me when she was pregnant, because she didn't believe in abortions. Funny how she didn't grasp that it would have been murder just the same had she forced a miscarriage. I guess it was meant for me to be here.

She never considered my feelings when she told me that. So many times in life, I wondered why she just didn't abort me. It would have saved me from all of this pain and misery.

I had not stopped wandering. I had wandered off to the pool one morning and when I came home, I walked into a drug raid in progress. I did not know what was going on, I came in and got on the ground with the rest of my siblings. When it was all over, the police officers allowed my sister to take the three of us younger ones and leave the house. Everyone else went to jail, including mom and my brother. She was released within the next day, my brother never was. When he was finally being released, my mom made no effort to get him.

We had two more drug bust before our house started to clear. Those people, our house guests were going to jail left and right. I was roving more frequently and later at night. I called myself having a job. I was working with an old African man doing absolutely nothing, just typing on a computer. I thought it was amazing because I had never seen a computer in real life. I was typing on a DOS screen.

It was around nine or ten o'clock p.m. and I told him that it was time for me to go. I started getting a bit nervous as he began to get closer and closer to me. He told me to come back the next day and we would set my schedule and decide on what he would pay me to work for him. When I got home that night, I was in trouble. It was strange to hear my mom yell at me for being out so late when I had been doing it for years. I guess she was sober and hadn't noticed when she was high. Whatever the case may be, it probably saved me from a sexual predator. Why in the hell would that man want me working for him, and why so late at night? I never went back. After telling my mom about my job she nearly lost her mind.

She was the most awesome mom when she was not on drugs. We always came first. We were clean, fed, and well kept. When mom was high, it was my eldest sister keeping me together when it was time for school. She was more like a mother to me. I don't ever remember my mom spanking me ever, but my sister did once, and it kept me in line. I didn't much care about the spanking. I was more worried about her being disappointed in me. I adored her, she was so beautiful. I use to brush her hair while she sang Anita Baker songs to me. She had a beautiful voice. I loved to hear her sing. Everyone did. I loved the fact that she took out time with me. She cared.

Throughout all of these happenings, I always made it a point to go to school. I loved school. I wanted to be a lawyer. I would get up on my own, dress myself, and make sure I got on the bus when my sister was not there to help me. Of course, my sister would comb my hair whenever she was around. Other times I was just happy to be nappy, as long as I was going to school. The kids didn't talk about me too much because I myself was a bit of a fighter. I had no problem kicking somebody's a**, boy or girl. I learned that from my brother and sister. They had given me pointers on handling my own when they were not around to fight for me. I prided myself on that. Nothing has changed. I have been fighting all of my life, just less and less as I got older, and my fights are no longer physical. Being vulnerable also took a bit of my fight away.

Here we go, the day we were taken away from my mom...

I had missed my school bus because I woke up late. I had done the same on several occasions and would freak out. I was bussed to a school more than fifteen miles away. Walking to school when I missed the bus, because I hated to miss school was becoming my usual form of transportation. I played the violin and it was my absolute pleasure. My music teacher told me that I couldn't play anymore if I was late to school again.

I could not risk that. I would not risk that!

I woke up late again. I missed the bus by seconds. I was not a happy camper and was determined to make it to school, on time. I was use to taking rides from strangers and decided to use my tears as a means to hitch a ride. I thought maybe someone would feel sorry for me and give me a ride. And they did!

Unfortunately, it was a school administrator. I don't know if you remember, but I said earlier that I would talk way too damn much, telling everything that goes on in my house. Well I did just that. My intentions were just to get to school on time.

I made it to school and right on time.

When I got home that day, the feeling in the atmosphere was somber. I had an eerie feeling that something was wrong. I knew something was wrong. I saw a police car as well as a car that was too rich for our blood, parked a few houses down. Even though they were not parked in front of my house, I just knew they were at my house. I did not go directly home. I walked around the block three or four times before going into the house.

When I got in the house, there was one cop, a white woman with my younger sister on her lap, my eldest sister holding my baby sister and me. I say white woman because Mamita was the only white woman that had ever been in our home. The first question I asked was, "Where is mommy?" My sister replied in tears, "In jail for fighting the police."

I knew then that my selfishness had gotten us taken away from my mother, I just never told anyone what I had done that morning to cause the school system get into my mother's business. My eldest sister was crying, she said, "They won't let me take you guys this time." That was the last time I saw her before she was murdered. She was a minor also. Maybe if they had taken her, she would still be alive. Maybe it was just her time to go.

CHAPTER ONE, VERSE ONE

CHAPTER 6

THEY SPELLED HER NAME WRONG

We were sitting at the table for dinner at Ms. Herring's house. Ms. Herring was our foster mother. Earlier that day, she had taken us out to rent movies. We were allowed to watch television during dinnertime because we had been so well behaved throughout the week. As we ate all types of weird food, something on the news caught my eye. This was the home where I met the girls that I spoke about in an earlier chapter in this book.

The News broadcast was showing footage of a popular complex called the G Parkway Apartments. The news anchor told of a tragic murder, describing two murder victims as male and female, ages eighteen and fifteen. I immediately got sick. I told Ms. Herring that it was my sister and her boyfriend. She was really upset with me and told me not to speak that way, ever. She explained that there was no way for me to be sure because the anchor had not given the names of the victims.

I could not speak at all. I had lost my appetite as well. I was sure that it was my sister and Marx. I held my tears in. I did not want to upset Ms. Herring.

Half an hour later, the doorbell rang. We were all so surprised. I was given instructions to go and answer the door. I was shocked and happy to see my mom, grandma, and aunt at the door. It might not have been my mother, but maybe her two sisters, but I cannot remember the details exactly. I was also confused. It was night and we were not allowed to have unauthorized visitors, especially at night, this was mandated by the foster court system.

I guess in my mind, I never thought that I would see real family again. I had already accepted this new life for what it was. I enjoyed the structure. I needed it.

My grandma had the hiccups, which usually meant she was extremely stressed out. She had the hiccups for days when my grandfather died.

Before I allowed them to sit down good, I started to explain to them what I heard on the news. I explained that the ages were the same as Marx and my sister.

My mom or aunt, in a very calm tone, said, "That was her baby."

My sister was dead.

The service was closed casket. She had been murdered execution style. One bullet in her back, upper right shoulder, and the other in the back of her head with her face carrying the location of the exit wound.

They spelled her name wrong on the obituary. That made me angry.

A POEM CALLED TRUTH

BY GINA GENELLE

People can't handle the truth. They have a hard time dealing with the freedom from deceit. Instead, they trust a lie, that one that defies all truth, having no real proof to sustain a sensible foundation, accepting self-degradation because it's comfortable. They never know what they are talking about, but always the first ones to shout, "I keep it real, I keep it real", Yeah, you keep it real alright, real dumb, and at night, it's from your demons you run. Where is your true lie now? You might as well throw in the towel and bow, like every knee shall anyhow. Oh, I forgot... "You ain't neva' scuurd" running around like your hard with no Word. That true covering and solid defense. When you read it, did you even understand what it meant?

Or was your time unbeneficial, spent memorizing scripts to solidify how saved you act and look. Yes, you've done the book....superficially, You didn't fool me, I couldn't be mistook. Truth knows truth and recognizes unfamiliar spirits you know? So go ahead and continue to put on that show. God is the giver of all things, and when my heart sings, He hears it. He hears the confessions of my wrong, through my soul's song. He hears my lamentations, and my pleads, when my enemies have formed themselves against me. The devil is a liar, and I don't feel no ways tired, for greater is He that is within me, than that of he who is in this world. That is why I continually refuse to cast my pearls at the swine that continue to pine away at my calling,

My anointing, not believing that I am what you see, but remember that greater is He that is within me. Know Truth when it presents itself. Know that God will be who He wills to be, even if that means me... I may have been the one to bring the blessings that you prayed for, but you chose to ignore truth and accept deceit. The Word says "Likewise, these filthy dreamers defile the flesh, despise dominion, and speak evil of dignities, but these speak evil of what they know not, but of the things they know naturally as brute beast. In those things, they corrupt themselves." We all need help! That is why we are to love each other as we love ourselves, then Christianity would be an easy sale, for this battle is won, successfully through the Son, Jesus!

And when the lie comes against trust, He believes us. Jesus is truth, let me be his proof, get to know me without judgment, for that time has not yet come. Yes, the battle is over, but with me, He is not done. "Touch not my anointed and do my profits no harm." Don't be alarmed, that's my only good luck charm. Why are you still searching for my truth when it is all up in your face? You keep shooting empty darts with haste, thinking it's a façade you'll erase. That ain't the case. I ain't on a paper chase nor am I in line for the next man. Its God who's holding my hand. Don't take my kindness for weakness, I was sent to teach this. Love comes from above, there is no unity in division, that choice was yours, you made that decision.

Let's all keep it real, God is watching still, waiting on one of us to get it right. I don't know about you, but I ain't going down without a fight. I put on the whole armor of God, as I tread the sod in this land of the lost, knowing that Jesus is boss, He is my access behind the veil, It's where I send my spirit to dwell, on my behalf. I know you don't understand, but I've embraced my past. It's where my life's lessons come from, growing my faith and belief in God's Son, edifying this body, 'til we become one. My spiritual authority, getting to know more of me, and just when the devil thought he tore me... I rise again, you see. Christ is my example. Be prepared because I am a handful, just like a tree planted by the rivers of water, bringing forth fruit in its season, salvation being my reason. Crying out to God for His people are suffering for the lack of knowledge. Not the stuff we learn in college for the very elite, but the real stuff that we learn in life and on these streets, the things that allow us to hate and be loved again, in spite of our sins.

And with the spoken Word utilized as a vessel to carry our faith, We have been given the ability to create, speaking those things as if they were, and casting out things that try to detour the calling of the Most High.

Never daring to ask why…

I AM THAT I AM

That's what He said, as we are the body and Him our head. Learn to handle it, handle the truth. He died on the cross and that's our proof.

THE BEGINNING OF A NEW END

CHAPTER 7

AN OLD FASHIONED MESS

We were moving into this big house on the west side of Los Angeles, 6 children, 3 boys, and 3 girls. This was a big come up, seeing as how we had come from the eastside where our housing was meagerly accommodating.

This was my Mamita's goal for us. It was explained to me that my aunt was getting a larger house to accommodate my great grandmother, sisters and I, unfortunately, Mamita passed away before she had the opportunity to live in the home.

The strange part about it is that she followed me there. I always felt and saw her presence for the first month or so of us residing in that house. It was as if she was trying her best to offer me some type of guidance, some comfort in knowing that she was still with me.

I wish I would not have, but I pushed her away. I was always told that it was a demon and that the spirit of a person returns unto the god that gave it. I was under the impression that I was being haunted by a demon, so I denounced it.

We believe in angels, so now I am somewhat perplexed about why it could not have been a guardian angel, taking form of one I could have easily accepted without fear.

I started my period prior to moving to Los Angeles and having to be cared for by my aunt. I had taken all instructions from the tower, the tower being Mamita. Most military personnel will understand the meaning of taking all instructions from the tower. The coined turn of phrase has become a part of my jargon as well as other phrases that you will probably encounter throughout the context of my writing.

Anyway, Mamita was very, very, very.....Old Fashioned. She would still refer to my sisters and me as "Gal" and often would ask what was "ailing us."

"What ailing you gyal" is how it sounded. (I am laughing aloud) It still sounds as country as hell to me. I often say the same to my daughters and they look at me as if I have lost my darn mind.

I know I keep getting off the subject, so let me regroup. I am still chuckling.

Okay... I bought up the subject of my great grandmother being old fashioned because of how she responded to me having my period. She had me thinking that I could die. (Laughing)

Maxi pads? What was that? How about towels and tissue?

She made me use towels, and she would wash them out with her bare hands. How gross? She also kept me out of school. I did not mind staying home, but the problem was that I had to stay in bed lying on my back all day. She kept hot compresses on my head and belly and would not allow me to bathe. Only showers were allowed. She said that the hot water in the tub would give me blood clots. She explained that I had become a woman. I translated this as meaning; I could not play anymore. I had to be responsible now. Therefore, I began to take more responsibility in teaching as well as spanking my younger sisters. I thought that was what adults did, tell people what to do and spank. I am sure my sisters didn't like it much, but I would have preferred me spank them than anybody else. After all, they were my responsibility as an adult.

"IM PRETTY SURE NOTHING GOOD COMES FROM THE HOOD"

My aunt hated that I had so much responsibility for my sisters. Once she took that from me, she began to have a hard time getting my sisters to conform to her standard and they would still come to me for everything. I felt as if she had drawn a serious wedge between us. Our relationships will never be the same. I know that my struggles are not theirs, and they do not remember a lot of what had taken place in our lives. I think they also feel as if I could not possibly remember either. Nevertheless, I do, the residue of it all lies buried under a thin layer of my skin and surfaces every time I scratch an itch.

God I love my sisters and during that time, we were inseparable. The three of us slept in the same twin sized bed, with each of us having an arm around the others neck. My position was always the middle. I needed to ensure that they both received the same amount of love from me. They were all that I had left.

Living with my aunt was my trial just as it was my mother's trial. She always looked at me in such a strange way, so demeaning. She made sure that I would never be confident. Now in all fairness, I really do not know what she was thinking. I have not a clue of how she actually viewed me. I can only explain how I perceived it, and how it has affected me.

She looked at me the same way she looked at the people at my sister's repast. She walked in with her fur on, as debonair as she wanted to be. She wouldn't sit when offered, and when she did, she acted as if her clothing was too clean to touch the chair. I thought she was rich.

For some reason, she could never separate me from her thoughts of what she considered to be beneath her. She did not believe that anything good came from the hood. What she didn't know was the hood did not raise me, I raised myself. I taught myself to be poised and confident even in the face of adversity. I never saw what I look like on the outside. I had been building who I was on the inside for years.

I used the television to develop who I was to become. I knew my outer appearance was that of a lowlife, but I was working from the inside out.

I was THE COSBY SHOW, I was Clair the lawyer, and my husband was a doctor. I was PUNKY BREWSTER, and was certain to find my Henry. I was RAGS TO RICHES. This little poor girl was bound to have fortune. I was the little ORPHAN ANNIE, literally.

I was to develop a sense of class from soap operas. I was going to marry a rich white man who would love me with the same intensity that those men on GENERAL HOSPITAL loved their wives. I was Laura and I was going to have a Luke for myself. I was Janet Jackson in the cast of FAME, dancing my way to stardom. I was also Janet Jackson as Penny, reminded that I was just a physically and emotionally abused child and Willona was going to save me from my misery. I was the JEFFERSON'S and was bound to move on up.

My aunt did not know that I had separated myself from all that was going on in my mother's home and was determined to be successful.

I played instruments, I won a citywide spelling bee, and I could miss weeks of school and never miss a beat academically. I was a smart girl with dreams. I just needed a push in the right direction. I needed support.

She could not see pass my rags. She could never see success in me, because I was my mother's daughter. In her eyes, I would be pregnant and thirteen years following, I would be a grandmother.

I once had an uncle tell me that I would be a grandmother in thirteen years. He told me this the week my daughter was born, not taking into consideration that I was turning twenty years old. I am glad he did though. It kept me focused and in tuned with my daughter. She is thirteen now and still no sign of a grandchild. What is even crazier is that if she were to have a baby at a young age, God forbid, I would give her all the support she needs to be successful. She is my child, and that is what mothers should do. Who gives a damn what anyone else thinks. Society's opinions have been known to destroy families. It would be just as much my fault if she were having sex at this age. It would mean that I failed to educate her properly about her body and relationships. I would have failed to explain to her the differences between love and lust and that proper decision making and love are contrary, one to the other. If this were to happen to her, I would have failed her, just as the adults in my life had failed me.

All the same, my aunt had no clue of what I had experience prior to coming to live in her home, she never asked either. She did not realize that all I had experienced advanced me years beyond my age, and I just wanted to be a child. I wanted a normal life.

She could only speculate and pass judgment based on the rumors she heard or pure assumption. She never cared enough to ask what I had gone through or if I was okay.

She never saw me. Nor did she know me.

Furthermore, when she did get a glimpse, she tried her best to break me down. It was too late. I was already broken.

Through this experience, I have learned that you never ever break a person down without building them up again. I continued to smile and laugh straight through the hurt. I have not lost that ability. It kills my enemies to see me smile when they have done all to cause me to fail. What is more important is that my laughter and smile is genuine. I have never lost that. There have been periods of my life when I lost the ability to shed a tear. I could not cry if I wanted to, but I have always maintained the ability to smile. As a matter of fact, I could not shed a tear at Mamita's funeral. A tearless cry is the worst type of cry. It is almost like being dead inside. I can understand the term Dead Man Walking from a very different perspective.

I spoke very proper and my views of life were always different. My thought process was not what she expected to come out of the lifestyle that I was living in. I was supposed to be ghetto acting. When I started to speak slang, she would criticize that. It never mattered that I practice hard to fit in. Everything I did was a problem.

My aunt could not fathom that maybe I was worth something. Instead of believing it, she called me a great fantasizer, she would say that I had a vivid imagination and that I was a big liar. Just because she could not see life as I did, I had to be lying. How could she say I was lying about something that she never experienced?

I tried hard not to view her as being beneath me. However, morally, she would never be on my mother's level. That is fact, not many were. My mother was a loving, giving, kind, and an honest woman, always. Even throughout her addiction, she never turned anyone away. She would give you the clothing from her back. Do not get me wrong, she did not take any sh*t from people. She would curse a person out, and in the same breath ask them if they were hungry. Her intent was not to hurt you, but she had to speak her mind.

Mamita told my aunt that there was something special about me. She told her to take care of me. I heard her. She did the exact opposite. I lived in pure hell. I would have rather grown up in the foster care system. I just could not bear to be separated from my sisters. I think what is so special about me is; I see everything special, especially in everyone else.

While calling me a liar and making a spectacle of me throughout the family, I humbly allowed her to do it. She had no freaking clue that this little girl had made it through a long stretch of life on my own.

I was also a fighter, if only she knew, had I defended myself every time she put her hands on me, I would have beaten her a**. However, my mother taught me to always respect my elders. I wish she would have expressed that there is a limit. In addition, I could never be the monster that she was trying to make me out to be. I was not that person. She never once tried to get to know me. She still doesn't know me, but I know her all too well.

Here was my take on the matter. I had come from a hurtful place. I had lost my mother to drugs, my sister to drug dealing and murder, and my brother to jail. All I had left was my sisters and one last opportunity to live a normal life. Understanding her thoughts was impossible. If she thought I was so screwed up, why didn't she get me some professional help?

She would beat me in my face and pull me by my hair, slinging me around the kitchen with my hair. Sorry, I get quite emotional just to think about the things she did to me. But there is no wonder why I keep a short haircut. I cannot give reason for why I was in trouble all the time.

Maybe I was beaten because her husband was molesting me. Maybe I was called a liar so that no one would believe me if I told.

They just watched, the family just watched. I don't care how bad she said I was. I didn't deserve that. Did they see my pain? Could anyone see my tears? Why wouldn't any one help me?

She would make things up about me and beat me for what she made up. The things that were not fabricated were so exaggerated. Her sons were bad as hell and way too disrespectful, but she would never lay a hand on them. There is not a time that I can remember. Every now and again my sisters would be spanked. I wished I could take the spanking for them. But it was mainly just me, and I was beaten and not spanked.

I was never disrespectful. In fact, I tried everything in my power to please her. Nothing was ever good enough.

My mom never spanked me and now I was getting beat on. What the hell? Was this God?

I didn't and still don't really understand why I have had to endure so damn much. I am crying profusely as I am writing because the pain of it all never goes away. Time does not heal all wounds. We just adjust, and adapt if we are strong, we use past pain to better ourselves. A constant reminder of what we will not endure or force upon another.

I do not know if there is or will ever be any real relief for me. I am still trying to figure out what I did to deserve it all. I know there are others who have experienced worse, but I can only speak of my pain.

Why didn't my mother just abort me?

TIME TO PUT MY FACE ON

When I got to school, I was who I wanted to be to a certain extent. I still had to put on a face to fit in. I had to take off the hurt face and slap on happy. I had friends, people to talk to, and no drama. I always loved school. It was my get away. I was free from stress until my last class.

It was all a façade. I was so unattached mentally and emotionally. I was popular because I could not stay with one group of people for too long. I liked everybody, but nobody at all, concurrently. It was just until I got home. I am not, nor have I ever been a people person. Now I am good at being social. I am an awesome conversationalist, if I must say so myself. I am tactful. I have natural leadership ability, but I was so use to being by myself. I could not handle when people would change. One minute they liked you, the next they did not. They talked about you behind your back and smiled in your face. I was not accustomed to this. I did not partake in this type of behavior, and when I did, it was just a show for whoever was around. I was more into writing short stories and passing them around. I was intrigued by how fast my writing got around school. I enjoyed the fact that I had gotten request for more stories. I have grown to realize that I have a hard time dealing with people, because I have no gray area. I am either black or white. There are no in- betweens with me, maybe a little red when I'm angry. I do not allow people to know that very often. I maintain my nicety, but I just will not tolerated being in their presence for too long. Otherwise, I speak my mind in a manner that stings. I've grown to realize that no matter how tough I try to be or sound, I am really just extremely emotional with a wall so high that oftentimes I cannot see over it.

    Sixth period was always the worse. I could not focus. I was too worried about if I had done anything wrong that day, I was worried about whether or not I was going to get pounded when I got home. I was afraid. Every time I would enter the house, I would ask my sister if my aunt was mad, not that I had done anything wrong, but I was sure to take the beating for whatever had gone wrong. I felt like I was her target. She based her whole existence around me. I was her focus, and not in a positive way.

OLD CHESTER THE MOLESTER WAS BACK, JUST IN NEW SKIN

Now, I did have all that I could want, as far as materialistic things. She made sure we had the best of everything. We were well dressed, but only because it was a direct reflection on her. She could not look like a million bucks and have us looking like orphans. It would make her look bad. We had to maintain that we were a "Holy" household. It had to look that way regardless of the mess that was taking place inside.

On top of getting my a** beat, my uncle was molesting me. He started doing this from the time I reached my aunt's house. Now by this age, I knew it was wrong. I just didn't know how to stop him. He would do my hair in my aunt's salon and have me stand up instead of sitting down. As he would do whatever he was doing to my hair, he would constantly rub his erect penis on my butt. It made me feel dirty. I hated that I had to accept it. He must have thought that I was enjoying it because I never tried to stop him or suggest that I did not want him to do that to me. I was an easy target. I was programmed not to tell.

In front of people, he would swear that I was not a virgin. My aunt even took me to the doctor to verify it. I did not need a checkup. She wanted to confirm that I was indeed a virgin. That was probably the only thing she believed was true about me. Nevertheless, I guess not, if it had to be confirmed by a doctor.

My uncle would ask me if I wanted to learn to drive, what teenager didn't? I just didn't know he was going to make me sit on his lap. I nipped that in the bud right away. I could control that. Outside of that, I couldn't stop him because I was afraid to tell. Whom would I tell? If I told, would they separate me from my sisters? If so, who would be there to protect them from him? I sacrificed myself. I figured I could handle it as long as he was not having intercourse with me. I would just avoid it as much as I could.

He would come into my room and wake me up for school in the morning. The way he did it was unconventional. He would rub his hands between my legs. I would jump, and he would pretend to be waking me for school. God! I prayed so hard. Why wouldn't this stop?

I started locking my bedroom door. I got in trouble for that, I also sat and listened while my aunt would tell people that I locked my door because I was sneaking boys in. How was I to tell her that I locked the door to keep your damn husband out?

I contemplated telling her in front of her customers at the salon the next time she fixed her lips to lie on me. I wanted to embarrass the hell out of her the way she did me all the time. What would her customers think about her then? How would they feel to know their precious hair dressing Evangelist was a big fat liar who was destroying a child's life, while they sat back enjoying the gossip?

MY DEMONIC POSSESSION

This was around the time I started to rebel. I felt like I should give her a real reason to talk sh*t about me.

How ironic, when I started acting a fool, I didn't get into trouble. Now she was able to see the difference. She was creating a monster and she didn't even know it. I was fighting at school, being suspended. I started treating people the way she treated me. No beating followed. I got a tattoo at sixteen, actually, I got two, and she only knew about one. I got the second one immediately after her biblical lashing about marking and scarring my body. No beating followed.

I was only getting beat when she made things up, except when my grades dropped. She had a field day with that. A grade of C always turned into a fail in all her conversations, anything to degrade me.

Around people who loved me and refused to partake in any negative conversations about me, she would praise me. "That Gina is so smart," where was this coming from? She was so damn phony. I hated it. She was a hypocrite, and called herself an Evangelist. Here is what really killed it for me, she prayed and read the bible ALL of the time. I never actually saw it, but that was the impression. Where was God? Was God allowing me to go through all of this? Surely not any god I would willingly choose to serve.

She would swear I had demons in me. (Laughing) we were headed to bible class on a Wednesday night and I was in the back of my uncles van with a Walkman. She was mad at me that day for something. At this point, I was really starting not to give a damn. She looked in the back of the van and saw the one red light from the Walkman. She freaked! She began to grab her chest and hyperventilate, she said that I had a demon and my eyes were glowing.

EYES? (Laughing)

There was only one light on the Walkman. She grabbed my head and started praying this demon out of me. It took everything within me not to burst out laughing. Everyone in the van knew that I had the Walkman but her. That was an ongoing joke for a long time. We all said nothing, we just allowed her to perform her exorcism.

She asked me if I was a lesbian one night at the dinner table, while going through my personal things. I liking boys was a no go. Did she want me to be gay? I don't know what her malfunction was. I think it was really just dysfunction. I was not allowed to like boys but she was accusing me of a girl? Hmm... something was not right.

THINGS WERE GETTING OUT OF HAND

Now that I think about it, I was not allowed to do anything, no boys, no worldly music, and no music if it wasn't gospel, no friends who did not attend church, no movies, no homecomings, no proms, no pants, no earrings, no makeup, just me, Jesus, and a daily a** beating. Sounds like a cult to me. I'm just saying!

This was my first real lesson on life. No matter how beautiful a person is on the outside, how well dressed, or what style of Mercedes they drive, you must first consider what is in the very heart of that person. Sometimes the origin of a person's heart is black. Things don't make a person, nor does it determine success. The woman who in public was debonair and poised, picturesque in standing, was disturbed mentally. I often secretly referred to her as mother dearest. I still cry when I watch that movie because it hits so close to home.

I would wake up in the middle of the night freaking out, because my aunt would creep into my room and hide in my closet. I would pretend that I was asleep and pray to God for this to stop. I didn't understand why she did this. She would literally stand in my closet with the door cracked open just enough for her to see out of.

She even did this when my cousins were spending the night over. I am glad she did because otherwise no one would have ever believed me if I told them. She had everyone believing that I was the liar. I just simply told a truth no one was willing to accept. I guess the lie was more comforting.

My cousins woke up the next morning flipping out. They asked me if I had seen what my aunt did. Little did they know, I had to live with it almost every night!

I was in love with a boy named Keishawn Jacobs. I wrote his name all over my phone book.

Gina loves Keishawn...

My aunt found it and sent me to a psychiatrist.

Dang, now that I think about it, Keishawn does sound like a girl's name. Maybe she really thought I was gay. I don't have anything against a person's choice to be gay. If the person is a good person, I could care less about their sexual preference. (I thought I would throw in that disclaimer)

Anyway, it was the first and last time I went to a psychiatrist. I cried the whole way there. I kept screaming that I wasn't crazy.

Truth be told, I am a little crazy. I accepted it a long time ago. Who isn't? I think it is even crazier to live a life pretending that I don't have issues. Maybe it is just me, but I get that crap out of my system right away, it is what it is. How can I fix me if I can't admit that "me" is all screwed up? I say what I mean and mean what I say. That is the beauty of me. I embrace it. I love me even when no one else does. Now from the outside looking in, I could only image what people think about me. I have the tendency to deviate from what society calls the norm.

Anyway, I refused to talk to this person, the psychiatrist. I explained that I wasn't crazy and that it was normal for me to like boys at sixteen. She finally explained to me that seeing a counselor didn't mean that I was crazy, it would help me to sort out my feelings. I likes to talk, and if it could help me I was all for it. I talk a lot now. I tell all of my business to people. I know it sounds crazy, but it serves two purposes. The first purpose is that if I tell you everything about me so you will not have to guess. If there is anything said about me that I did not tell, 9 times out of ten, it is a lie or rumor, probably derived from a truth.

Again, people would prefer a lie. It just feels more like right. The second purpose is that it is free counseling. Once that mess is out of my system, I tend to feel a whole lot better. I could care less about what people do with what I told them afterwards. I cannot get angry because it is all true.

When I decided that I wanted to continue to see the psychiatrist, my aunt stopped taking me.

I am almost certain that my aunt realized that I might have told that person everything that was going on with me. She would have been in a lot of trouble for abuse. And their definitely would have been a sexual abuse case opened. Regrettably, I don't even think she thought that far ahead, I think her main concern was losing that extra income.

PROM NIGHTMARE

My aunt told me that if I went to my prom, she would not pay for any of it. However, if I went to my churches Grad night, she would pay for it. So I unwillingly agreed. I really had no other choice.

I told her that if I went to the Grad night, I wanted to be different from any of the other graduates. I wanted to be elegant.

She took me shopping to get my dress.

My hopes were of getting a green and black beaded gown. Of course, green is still my favorite color. I explained to her in detail, the style in which I would wear my hair. We could not find a green dress that would fit me. So I opted for black and gold. It turned out just as I had expected so I was happy. I had finally come to terms with the fact that I was not going to prom.

The day before my Grad night, I came home from school to find that my aunt was wearing the same exact hairstyle that I described to her. To add fuel to fire, she showed me her dress...

Yes, a green beaded gown!

I was pissed off!

I know that I specifically said that I wanted to be unique. This was my night and I wanted to be different. Why would she do this to me? I was in the salon going off. I was in tears. I asked her why she would do that. I didn't understand. She had already taken prom from me, why would she take the one night that would belong to me.

She had this smirk on her face as she told her customers that I was just jealous. Jealous?!

Can you believe this? I couldn't. This b***h had no clue. She didn't understand the torture she put me through.

That was it. I was done. I had to speak my mind, in front of her customers too. I was done with her.

I said, "Whatever, wear that dress, you will never look as good as I do in my dress anyways, so it doesn't matter"

Alas, the look on her face was priceless. I hit a nerve that humbled her a**. It humbled her even more when we got to the venue and everyone was complimenting me. They were telling me how elegant and beautiful I looked. I was sucking it up. I loved the dumbfounded look on her face. Her plan had backfired. She probably didn't mean any harm, but she had done so much damage to me that I couldn't tell if it was a good will gesture or if she was just antagonizing me. What pissed me off the most was that I felt bad for her. I was regretting ever saying such mean things. In the end, it didn't make me feel good to see her feelings hurt because of me. I tried to rationalize that she had brought it upon herself, but that didn't work. I was just not mean girl.

All those years she had told lies about me, and for the first time, I became what she was, in front of her customers. I had displayed weakness. I had never allowed anyone to see me respond to all that she had done until this day.

I didn't like the feeling of her being right about me.

I MEAN NO HARM

I really did not mean for this chapter to be about bashing my aunt. Nevertheless, this book is about my life and this is what it was for me. She was my demon. I have always wanted a stable relationship with my aunt, but how can I forgive her if she has never asked for forgiveness. Maybe she isn't sorry. I won't apologize if I don't feel as if I have done something wrong. I honestly think that she doesn't know that she has hurt me so badly. Maybe she doesn't care. No one has ever told her that she was wrong. I really need for her to apologize. Maybe I will forgive her anyways, with or without the apology.

I guess I am sort of venting in a way. (Therapy) I am sure there were some good things about her because everyone else loved her. I loved her. But then again, no one else had to experience the things that I have with her, except my mother.

It gets worse and there is more to tell but I will stop with this because I am becoming emotionally drained.

What I will say, is this, living with her hurt me more than any other hurt, I have experienced up until this point.

This would continue to affect the direction my life would take. I spent way too many years trying to live for her approval. I would fight myself so much. I was afraid to be who I am because I needed to prove to my aunt that I was not worthless. Who was she to be my judge? I really needed to prove it to myself because a part of me started to believe her. She made me feel worthless.

Now, I focus on pleasing myself because it is impossible to please a person who is unhappy with themselves, and most of us are.

I don't please people anymore. I praise them any opportunity I have. I have accepted the truth about me, and my faults. It is not easy, but I embrace who I am. I love me. Finally! I wish I had a magic stick to hit people with, so they can understand the lesson that I had to learn the hard way, with just one lick with my stick. I wish I could just give a hug and take the pain away.

Most people consider me a b***h now, family mostly. I will correct a person in a heartbeat if I feel as if they are putting me in a bad headspace. Now, I could care less about who does or does not like me. I will give to a person until I have nothing left. I will love you until my love is rejected and then some more. My heart is right and I genuinely love people, but I WILL NOT allow people to say just anything to me. I am not so passive anymore. Maybe it's just an unnecessary defense mechanism. Now I say exactly what I feel. I refuse to take hurt feelings to bed with me. I get it out right then and there.

Simply put, I treat people EXACTLY the way they treat me. They are just usually not strong enough to handle the very same things that they have just said to me. I become the bad person. I am okay with that because I hold no grudges but one. I mean no harm, but I believe that a person shouldn't dish it if they can't take it, a prime example of treat people how you want to be treated. I just enforce it. I am extremely nice to nice people and horribly mean to mean people, only after attempting to offer kindness.

I know it is hard for some to accept this Gina. I had to reintroduce myself. I used be very passive. I was sensitive. I would cry so many tears. I wanted people to like me. I knew if they took out the time to know me, and not determine how they felt about me based on what someone else told them, they would find that I am easy to love.

It hurt when people were mean. I knew that people were taking my kindness for weakness. I was never weak. Not many could have endured the things I have and still walk a straight line the way I have. Many have gone through worse, and I applaud you with all that is within me. It is not easy!

I often use truth about people to defend myself. When people begin to lie on me, I tell the truth on them. I believe that accepting one's self truth is the purest form of repentance.

I acknowledge my wrongdoing as soon as I recognize it. I accept it and work on positive change for the sake of self. Yes, I am selfish now, but how can I effectively help someone else if I am all jacked up? It doesn't work. I am working on me first, so that I can take my all and give it away.

Truth hurts. It is always easier for a person to point out someone else's fault, than it is for them to focus on self. I have had so many people try to fix me, "handle me," and all sorts of things because they don't like who I am, or would question, "Who do you think you are?" I am laughing, the question should always be, "Who do you say I am?" The determination belongs to you. I am that I am!

While they are pointing out my faults, I fix them, and then they get all upset because they never expected me to better myself. Now that I am better, they realized they spent too much of their time working on me and they are still all jacked up. Thank you!

I really hate to sound cocky, but some of the messages in this book are subliminal, I know that the people that I am actually speaking of are going to be nosey and read it.

I hate it when people say. "They are just haters and those haters are motivators." News flash... I am self- motivated. I have no need or room for the hater in my life and neither should you. Haters are not motivators; they are unhappy individuals with misguided notions that attacking others will make them feel better.

I figure if you don't like me, stay far from me and I will do the same. Happy, happy, joy, joy! See how that works?

I don't bother anyone. However, I will defend myself against an attack. On the other hand, what I deem an attack. It usually makes me the most hated person around, but if more attention were paid to the situation, they would realize that I was only defending myself.

As of lately, I have learned to choose my battles. Not every occasion constitutes the need for my attention. With that having been said, my beef is never the person, but the spirit[10] within them, their attributes. I understand that some people are just that way, but they must understand that this is my life, and I choose not to tolerate certain things in my life anymore.

I honestly believe that half the time people are clueless of the effect they have on people, and really don't understand why I respond the way that I do. This is probably just who they are and I demolish them mentally in a very articulate way. At first it was a defense mechanism, and then I realized I was just practicing or paying them back for all the times I didn't stand up for myself. That's wrong. I'm working on that.

I mind my own business. I figured the best advice is the advice that is asked for. I do not give advice unless it is requested of me or if the situation I find myself in warrants it. But what if it was necessary for me to go

---

[10] Ephesians 6:12-18 For we wrestle not against flesh and blood, but against principalities, against powers, against the rulers of the darkness of this world, against spiritual wickedness in high places.

through all that I've endured to be of service to someone who has or is suffering through similar situations?

I have to give accountability for my life, my life only. I am praying that I do the right thing. I pray that the words of my mouth and meditation of my heart is acceptable to God, even when others cannot see it.

A POEM CALLED NAKED

BY GINA GENELLE

I rest naked, in celebration of me. Not this physical being, but the spirit within.

No need to pretend that this body so wicked, could house such perfection, who would have predicted?

I am He sent, She sent, knees bent offering praise, submitting my life for the rest of my days.

I have been chosen, like a golden apple on an oak peach tree, walking in the calling God has crafted for me.

Celebrating life, love and learning, but life eternal is what I am yearning

06 April 2010

BEFORE THE FALL

CHAPTER 8

WHY IS OUR GOOD ALWAYS EVIL SPOKEN OF?

I lived in an upstairs apartment with my mom, her husband, and my two eldest siblings. I was the baby at the time and I believe my mother was pregnant. My memories of this period are very stagnant. I know for sure that my mother's sister lived directly downstairs from us with my uncle and cousin.

Although we attended church a lot, I don't ever remember being there, with a few exceptions. I remember leaving for church and coming home. I can remember coming home so easily because it was never fun for me.

My mother's husband liked to play this game. He would act as if he didn't see me. My mother and me and siblings would join in.

"Where is Gina?" they would call out. "I am right here!" I would scream while crying. Was I there?

They would play this game for what seemed like forever. I was the only one not having fun. I did not think it was funny. I thought they really couldn't see me. No one ever made any real effort to comfort me after playing such a cruel game at the expense of my feelings.

I hated my mother's husband. My mother hated that word. She would tell us that hate was a strong word and that we should say that we strongly disliked a person place or thing. I hated him strongly. He always found a way to hit or pinch one of us while my mother was gone. He once hit me with a belt buckle and the majority of my pinky nail came off. It took years before it grew back.

However, my mother loved him I guess, but she loved everyone.

He was a mean man. He made it clear to me that he was not my damn father. On the other hand, I had my mom making me call him daddy. When I would say daddy while no one was looking, he would whisper to me, I am not your daddy. Therefore, I stop talking to him unless he spoke to me first. I could not have been more than two or three years old.

One afternoon the living room of our home was dark. I came out of my room because I heard noises. It was my aunt with her gun threatening my mom's husband as he held on to my mom's wrist as if she was a child. She was crying. I started to cry also because I didn't understand what was going on. I just knew it wasn't good. I saw very little of him after that day. I know for sure he didn't live with us anymore.

We moved quite a bit after that, there was a lot of instability, new places, and strange faces at every turn.

My mom was a woman of great faith. In fact, her faith was so great she didn't work. She trusted that God would make a way. Even to pay the utilities. The fanatical thing about it was that He always did. Now granted there were times that we did not have lights in the house, but it was never for long. Still throughout my mother's addiction she maintained her spirituality and faith in God.

I remember us moving and having to stay with my Mamita and my mother's uncle. I vaguely remember an argument between the two of them, my mom, and uncle. Mamita tried to mediate.

My uncle spanked us for eating. My eldest sister told my mom.

During this period, my mother was still heavy in the church. She was walking in the way of righteousness. She came home yelling at my uncle. She asked him how he could hit on her babies when he doesn't even hit his own kids.

She explained that she bought that food and if her babies wanted to eat they could. He kicked my mom out, Mamita was upset, and she said that my mom didn't have to leave. My mom told her that she loved her and refused to be anywhere that her children were not welcomed.

We had a stable life at first until whatever issues my mom and her husband had. That was when everything went downhill. The next thing I knew, we were moving out of town.

I talked to my mom as an adult trying to figure out why the drastic change in our lives. I told her that I remembered a time when everything was so normal and peaceful. Her simple explanation was, "The church."

She told me how after her fight with my uncle, he went and told the pastor that it was my mother's intent to live with people without paying any rent. He painted a picture to the pastor, of my mother as being a user. She said that the pastor announced her dismemberment with the church in front of the entire congregation, warning them of her alleged intent. The intent that was shared with the pastor after the fight my uncle and mom had.

My mother said that the pastor not once asked her what was going on or what happened. He just took my uncles word for it.

No one ever took into consideration that she was going through a tough time with four kids. She had obviously lost her husband and her baby girl almost died. She needed help. I could have sworn it was the church's responsibility to help people. Instead, they pushed her out. The outcome was all of the perils we had to face.

My mother loved God until the day she died. The church destroyed her. Why?

Although she had the freedom of choice, do we not hold a responsibility as the church to take care of each other? Are we our brother's keeper?

LOVE AND LIFE, OR SO IT'S CALLED

CHAPTER 9

ON MY OWN, AGAIN

I was eighteen and on my own, finally freed from the hell I had been living in, not knowing that I would encounter much worse situations.

Prior to turning eighteen, I had considered the fact that I would no longer be living in my aunt's house. She had given me plenty of fair warning. She made sure I knew that she was not going to have a grown woman living in her house and not being paid for me. I understood totally.

So, I enlisted in the Navy, following my older cousin's example. I saw that he had made a success of himself. He was probably the best example that I had in my life. I was scheduled to leave July 19, 1995, the month following high school graduation.

The recruiter screwed me. Thank goodness, my cousin was in town to go over my classification paper work. He was not happy, told me to get dressed. We were going to see my recruiter. I was scared sh*tless. I had no clue of what was going on. I thought I was good to go.

We got to the recruiter's office, and well, have you ever heard the term cursing like a sailor? My cousin gave him the business. He told him that he needed to get my stuff straight. He also told me, right in front of the recruiter that I did not have to go. I had only sworn in once and could change my mind if I wanted to. You had better believe I changed my mind. I got the hell out of dodge when 19 July 1995 rolled around.

Outside of that, I knew that I was going to need a job to survive. I wasn't allowed to work, so I had no experience. I obtained my social security and birth certificate on my own without my aunts knowledge, for just in case. The one good thing about the foster care system is that they attempted to prepare you for the transition into adult hood. They taught me how to interview and write resumes. They explained things to me I never would have learned at home.

I never needed any experience because I was a hell of a writer, I thought. I wrote all types of things into my resume. All of it was true, just embellished a little bit, for example; budgeting. My ten-dollar allowance hardly constituted accounts payable and receivable, but it worked as a viable skill.

I got by. I was cheated, and mistreated by people whom I called friends. I did not have an expectation of people to do things to me that I would have never done to them. I guess this is what my aunt meant by me being different from the rest of the world. She was right.

I had no social skills. I had never been allowed to go to the movies or hang out with friend outside of school. I was not even allowed to go to my prom.

I have been successful in many things in life. My accomplishments thus far supersede all that has been expected of me by many people. I am not done yet. I am just getting started. My pass is my motivating force. I PRAY OFTEN THAT MY STORY WILL MOTIVATE OTHERS TO DO THE SAME. I try not to boast, but sometimes you have to be your own champion. Sometimes you are all you have to make it through from one day to the next. The power of life and death lies in the tongue. It is important to speak life into existence.

I GRADUATED

I woke up alone and naked in a motel room, he had left me there. I am guessing that he left me, assuming that I was dead.

When I was in the Sheriff's Academy, I was told by a coroner during a certain block of training, that protruding blood vessels in the eyes of a dead person was a sign of strangulation.

I jumped up in a panic, sore all over. Hours had passed from the time I last remembered.

It all started because I was yelling at him, I called him a punk, and told him he was weak. I wanted him to leave me alone. Why were we even there?

When he balled his fist to hit me, my first reaction was to fight back. I whaled on his a** as if my life depended upon it. I pulled hair, punched and scratched. I displayed the true essence of fighting like a b***h. I didn't care. He was 6 feet, 5 inches and I didn't have a chance. I 5 feet, 3 1/2 inches, but there was going to be evidence that his a** had been in a fight.

He over powered me and wrapped his large hands around my neck. He squeezed so tight that I could not breathe. I kept trying to tell him that I could not breathe. I remember the moment my lips started to stammer and tears rolled down my eyes. I woke up alone and naked.

I looked in the mirror and didn't recognize myself. My mouth was busted and my eye was swollen damn near shut. There was a busted blood vessel in my eye. It is still partially visible 'til this day. All I could see in that mirror was my mother. I guess I had finally graduated past molestation to rape. It was 2 months before my nineteenth birthday.

I was pregnant.

TURNED ON BY THE IDEA OF LOVE SHORT LIVED

I just wanted to be loved. I wanted to be with someone who would love me unconditionally and have no real expectation of me loving them in return. I needed a man that understood that I don't know how to truly feel love for a man. I just wanted to feel loved by one. I have never been loved by a man. I was good at expressing what I believe love is. I just could never really feel it for a man. In my mind, all men have always wanted one thing from me. I guess I have always given off some type of sex vibe. My aunt would call it a lust demon.

I had an idea of love, so I put on a good show. I would go through the motions. I knew how to treat a man. I was the perfect woman in my eyes. I would provide an illusion of perfection just to feel a superficial love.

It never mattered much to me that it wasn't real, it just felt good for the moment. As long as I felt love, I could continue playing house. When that love ceased to exist, I know longer desired to be with the man. I always know that my relationships will not last; I just ride them through until all possibilities have been exhausted.

I could stroke an ego as well as other things that needed stroking just the same.

These situations were few and far in between. My first priority was my daughter. I am a mother and provider first.

I was a go-getter, I didn't need a man for money, and I always ended up with a broke a** man.

I just wanted a man that could provide me with a stable foundation and I could handle the rest from there. I was unsuccessful. I kept choosing the wrong men. I didn't want to be considered a gold digger so I would choose men that had nothing and expected to live off me.

That was an absolute No/Go[11]. I already felt like I was climbing a ladder with my daughter on my shoulders. I would be pulled down faster than I could pull someone up, especially a grown man.

Every time I offered my love, I would get nothing in return. I finally realized what my problem was. I was a hopeless romantic. For real, I was really hopeless, and so were the men that I had chosen for myself. I have always known that true love existed, but there were stipulations for that, stipulations that I was not willing to disclose to any man.

[11] Not in a suitable condition for proceeding or functioning properly

I do not, nor will I ever trust a man with my heart completely. Ever, never, ever. Amen! God will have to do some serious heart surgery, because mine is broken.

But then again, I am not sure a man could ever really trust me completely. I would not give 100% because of my lack of trust. A man would never know I didn't trust him. I am good at concealing certain emotions while freely expressing the one's I feel are important to keep a man occupied until he is ready to move on.

It is actually hard for me to feel anything but pain. Hurt has been the only consistent emotion throughout my stretch of life. It seems that I learn more through hurt and pain than when I am settled. I have survived so long that I have not yet learned how to live again.

My favorite emotion is love. I do believe that love is an emotion. It comes and goes just like happiness and sadness. They say God is love. If that is the case, I am right on track because I am even uncertain about God at times. Not to say that He is non-existent, but to say that I am not sure of who or what He really is. I feel the same way about love.

I believe in love at first sight. I have absolutely felt in love with a man at the sight of him. I got butterflies and all. It lasted about 15 minutes, but it was the greatest 15 minutes in that whole day.

DON'T GO BREAKING MY HEART

I allowed myself to truly love one man and he was careless with my heart. Most of the men that I have encountered have been. I just cared for real this time. I knew it would happen, but he had been hurt and I didn't want to be the next to hurt him. So I sacrifice me for him. I allowed him to see what genuine love felt like. I fought for him, I begged, I pleaded. I really felt something for him. He could care less.

As I always do, I got over it. He was easy to get over because I knew that if the love were not reciprocated, I would lose interest. I did give him my all, everything but my trust. I really wanted us to work.

A POEM CALLED
FOR YOU
I WILL
BY GINA GENELLE

Not my Sun, but the bright exuberant light that precedes it.

It is my confidence, eluding the thought of avoiding to embrace the warmth of being in your heed.

The panic that chases me into a retreat, too many miles the distance from our true destiny's resting place.

It is the trust that I have fruitfully assembled walls about, so sarcastically, to encamp its refuge

It is the sanctuary in which my love is housed beyond the veil.

It is the trail of oddments scattered strategically, that tell tales of a once whole heart scorned, torn to pieces by tragic misfortune

It is the faith that haunts my yearning to remain in disbelief, finding comfort in being deceived by things that are tangible.

It is the strength in your voice that comforts my hesitation

The knowledge you behold that curtails my unjustified apprehension, the arms you offer while holding me.

It is the audacity I liberate to tell you finally… I love you It is the ease in which I relinquish those words It is the difficulty in which I allow you to love me in

return.

06 April 2010

THE TIE THAT BINDS

I got married. He was okay. When the love was good, it was good. Damn it when things were bad, they were ugly. He was a dog. He not only cheated on me, he beat me and raped me. I know they say a man cannot rape his wife, but no means no. Love should never hurt that bad.

He tortured me. He also had a baby with another woman while I went away to fight in the war. I was focused on fighting for my country during Operation Enduring Freedom, and my husband was using his freedom to make a baby.

That didn't really hurt me much, what hurt was that I had no assistance with our kids. I was honestly glad that he had become someone else's headache. She thought she had a prize. She sat on the phone with me telling me how she was going to be there for my husband. I didn't feel sorry for her at all. I felt that being with him was punishment enough for her. She did not need me yelling at her. I wished her luck and moved on with my life. Her five-minute relationship with him could never compare to the ten plus years I had to endure his wrath. She could have him.

If it had not been for my husband's mom, I would have probably lost my kids to the system while I was fighting in a war as a single mother and soldier. His youngest sister was also an angel in my life.

I stayed with him only because of my daughter. She was the tie that binds. He thought that I was so naïve. He took submissive for stupid. I tried to explain to him that the two are not the same. Just like bullshit and reality are not the same. He just did not get it.

He took advantage of me every chance he got. He had no remorse for the things he did to me. He told me that he slept with my best friend. He was just uncivilized.

The greatest thing about him was his love for the kids.

Unfortunately, love doesn't pay child support. He never helped me.

He tried, just like my aunt to break me down. After I finally left him, He said to me, "Your strong yo, no one is gonna be able to break you".

It really freakin' hurt to know that it was his intent to break me. I will never understand it, but I am still smiling and carrying on with life. All that he did to break me caused me to strive harder to succeed.

He never made it in one night. Why did I even ask why? He was with one of his friend who was a sweet man on the surface, but I knew he was giving his girlfriend the same headache.

I must have questioned him one time too many and triggered him. Alternatively, he was just using it as an excuse to maintain his "Rude bwoy" reputation in front of his friend.

He was not a bad man. I saw straight through him. He did things because he wanted everyone to believe he was bad. He wanted to be respected for being greater than he really was. What good is respect if it has not been earned? Respect is earned, not given.

He could not decipher the difference between fear and respect. He scared people and embraced their fear as if it made him feel powerful. I was never scared of him. I was afraid of his ignorance. I feared the measures in which he would go to be acknowledge as a bad boy.

He was a punk in reality. I had only really seen him scare woman, his mother, his sisters, and I.

I had only heard him tell tales of what madness he created. To me he was just a mamma's boy who wanted so desperately bad to be accepted for all the wrong reasons. She supported his nonsense every step of the way. He knew she would continue to bail him out, so he continued with his crap.

When I had asked him one time too many, where he had been the night prior, he put a chrome pistol to my head, finger on trigger. His friend begged him to stop. He pleaded with him telling him to consider the fact that his baby girl was sitting in my lap. He made me strip down to nothing and removed every article of clothing that I owned from the house to keep me from leaving him. He only did this to make sure I was home when he came to apologize for what he had done to me.

Even though in his mind, it was just a show he put on for his friend, he didn't consider that it was my head and life on the other end of that loaded gun. He never considered the possibility of an accidental shooting, nor did he consider my baby would have been in my lap when her father killed me. He also never thought about the fact that my eldest daughter was also in the house.

This situation seems drastic, but it is the very least of many that I suffered while married to him.

War was going to be a cakewalk for me.

WHAT I MUST DO TO REALLY LOVE AND BE LOVED, BUT YET UNWILLING

I know that if I want to ultimately love and be loved. I have to do the unthinkable.

I have to humble myself. I recognize that love is not for me. Let me explain…Love is for me to give, not just the expectation to receive it.

I have to truly love me, in order to give love to anyone else.

A POEM CALLED HUMBLED

BY GINA GENELLE

It is funny...

I always scream about how I am a humbled woman. How unselfish I am.

It is also funny...

How I am immediate with my action to criticize without realizing that I have disregarded my own faults, existing as if I only, am well taught...

As if I have brought the bulk of our solidity to the table.

But what I have truly done is enable myself to uproot my bits and pieces, and have become unstable, unable to fathom life without you. Giving you what you require to grow while I continue to put on a show, performing as if I believe that I can live well without the two and this is all me, and none of it is you.

Screaming about how I can't stand the self-righteous, when I am the tightest in the game. And it's a damn shame that I have been blessed with many things but have been blinded and refuse to see… See the truth behind what it is that you really mean to me.

I call you my man because you are forcing me to become the woman I am supposed to be. Forget a college degree or any type of education, you have broken me down to the lowest frustration and I keep casing the joint like I am about to rob a brother, when I have been the sucker that's being robbed all the while, allowing myself to stress about not carrying our child.

Shame on me and that's my verdict, that was sorry of me and from me you heard this.

God told me, He advised me ahead of time that you were for me, gave me ample time to prepare to be who I wanted to be. But I had to have you now, so selfish of me.

Didn't care how, the why's or the when's, but never expecting my life to take this spin. So quick to blame, taking no responsibility, I asked for this, but always the one ready to flee.

Although I love you to death and sustain the ability, had to release my eyes to what I was powerless to see. You are for me and me for you, but these things we must continue to go through constantly our reality, inch by inch bringing out the child in me.

I never learned to live but only to survive.

I forgot how to survive but learned how to run, tried to bail out when things weren't as fun. Such is life and I am learning to adjust, to put my faith in God and to offer you my trust.

So humble am I? Well let me see...

I couldn't define it so pulled out the dictionary. To my surprise, I was on the wrong path and because of my pride, doing all the wrong math.

Professing to the world how unwilling I am to lower my standards and won't settle, priding myself on it as if it were a Gold medal.

After reading the definition on humble, It was like a slap and I had to face it, I found all I had built was just more time wasted.

This caught my attention and grabbed my heart. This truly humbled all that I considered smart.

It said that I was to reduce to a lower standing in my own eyes. Well hell if that didn't come as a surprise to me, and shook my spirit like an old rag doll. Took a deep breath 'cause I had to pause for just a moment to take this all in, but when I read further my head started to spin.

I was to debase, degrade, demean, discredit, disgrace, dishonor, humiliate, lower, shame myself???

Oh my God please send me some help. So all this time I thought I was humble, I had been humbling others. This was some real undesirable knowledge to discover...

How could I have been submissive to you, without being humble?

So I have been bringing you nothing but trouble? Baby for this, I truly apologize and will continue to pray that God makes me wise.

It was never my intent to cause you pain, and forever my love will increase and remain. Bear with me as I grow stronger, and understand that all that me, me, me is no longer. But two bodies with yet one soul, and sorry in advance for losing control of my actions at times, but unfortunately that won't stop till you are totally mine.

GOT ME LOOKING LIKE GOMER PYLE

CHAPTER 10

U. S. A R M Y (Uncle Sam Ain't Released Me Yet)

Mmm...

There is nothing sweeter than the sound of cadence at 0530 in the morning. Loud and proud! Who needs coffee when the cadence is so sweet?

Dress right, dress. Lottie Dottie, everybody!

I had a bit of experience because of my Sheriff's Academy Training. That made it almost inevitable that I would be Platoon Guide, two out of three phases of Basic Combat Training (BCT). I knew my s**t.

It also made BCT a breeze for me. The only thing I could not stand was the cold in Ft. Lost in the Woods, Misery. That is what we called it. It was actually Ft. Leonard Wood, Missouri. I could have served my whole army career in Basic Training, if only they got my black a** out of Leonard Wood.

I love uniformed services. In BCT, I was what they called Hooah. I could never stand that word. That word could mean anything. It was constantly abused. What it means to me and how I use it, are at two opposite ends of a spectrum. To me it means that a person is all or nothing for the Army, patriotic, and ready to defend at all cost. However, I used it to tell a superior "f**k you" without being disrespectful.

If a leader ordered me to perform a task that is within my scope of duty, I respond, "Yes, Sergeant." with respect and honor. If I am asked to perform unnecessary sh*t, I respond, "Hooah" with a smile and drive on. What I am really saying is "f**k you for making me do this stupid s**t Sergeant."

The problem was, I was a lot older, and more educated than most of my senior leadership. I was into working smarter and not harder. Most of these people were dumber than a box of rocks and did not take well to a woman who would out shoot and out P.T.[12] them.

People kept telling me to play the game, but I was in a very different mindset, I wasn't playing games. This was my life. Why should I have to settle for these peoples games because they felt I needed to act my rank? How was my rank supposed to act, hell, I was squared away. These kids, in my eyes had no life experience, nor work experience other than the Army. I had my sh*t together.

I was dress right f**king dressed.

"Get the freak Outta here with that bulls**t" was my mentality. I was a leader's worse nightmare. I still had that Cop mentality and knew my regulations inside and out, even when they didn't. I set a standard that they could not

---

[12] P.T. is physical training.

upheld. Who was I to make them look bad when I was just a f**king Private First Class? I am sure that was their thought. I heard it more times than I could count.

My intentions were to come in and wreck shop. I was going to be the toughest female soldier there was. I was, but that was a problem. I was a bit too tough. I was tougher than most men were and it became competitive instead of a team concept. I thought I was supposed to be tough, but they wanted me weak and submissive. I could not conform to that standard. I am a soldier got damn it! But for them, hat was the wrong answer; it was a No/Go.

Although I excelled at the Army Standards, I was sucking at being a soldier. I did not know how to play the game. I played by the regulations only. If it wasn't in the regulations, I was not going to conform. I was battling with leaders who were constantly challenging me. They hated me. (Laughing)

When they could not subject me to any form of Uniform Code of Military Justice (UCMJ), they started making things up. I became their target. During this time, I didn't learn anything viable to assist me through battle. My battle was with the people I was supposed to trust in war.

Although I was right about the regulations and won every time, I was wrong about the way I went about things. Now some situations warranted my fight and buck against the system, but others were just because I did not know how to stop fighting. I did not know how to choose my battles. I thought everybody was out to get me.

I felt that they didn't respect the fact that I was a single mother of two, who had to get up twice as early to comb hair and care for two children prior to P.T. all by myself. Why couldn't they respect the fact that I was still exceeding the standards with opposition on my shoulder?

I didn't have a spouse ironing my clothes and taking care of my kids while I did nothing but go to work and home to a prepared dinner. I had to come home and be a full time mother. I had to help with homework, cook dinner, do laundry, and give love as well as discipline, all while never failing to fulfill my responsibilities as a soldier. I felt as if their concerns were ill intended. In the end, I was the one who signed up for this.

I tried to find a balance but was unsuccessful for three years.

NO PEACE IN A TIME OF WAR

I love the Army. Joining the military has been one of the best choices that I have ever made for my life. It has afforded me the opportunity to provide a level of stability for my girls that I have never had for myself.

The standards of the Army are set up for success. Although, sometimes the people in the positions are ate the f**k up, it does not take away the prestige of the U.S. Army. The regulations are set up to not only protect, but also serve a greater purpose, other than just punishing soldiers. Poor leadership in any arena or workforce will decrease morale.

I have seen poor leadership cause soldiers to commit suicide prior to even making it to the battlefield. It is sad, but so very true.

I dare not blame the Army, but the person behind the rank for taking such little concern for the life of a soldier. Even more so, I blame the individuals who make it possible for these leaders to maintain such low standard. This generally occurs when leadership plays the battle buddy game, "I will help you because I like you." It causes all others to dwindle away in the system.

The individuals that are sacrificed are the soldiers who would make the greatest leaders, but refuse to play the game. They will not conform to a lower standard and are out cast with in their Units, denied all access to progression.

They say, "Sh*t rolls downhill," meaning the person at the bottom is usually the one being sh*t on. What they fail to mention, is that the sh*t is at the top. It stains everything it touches on the way to the very bottom. The bottom just suffers the most. The problem is that the soldiers at the bottom are not the sh*t. The leadership is the real sh*t. Soldiers just carry the sh*t.

This is not true for all leaders. There are those few great leaders that produce other great leaders.

Upon arrival to my first Unit, I was given a three- month warning of my deployment. I was having a hard time settling in with the girls.

My mother and father, the man I called dad, had died prior to my entrance into the Army. In addition, I had just separate from an abusive marriage. I just needed a little time to be grounded.

Instead, I was faced with constant flirtation from senior leaders and even propositions. Although I hate to say, some females used it to their advantage. I refused. This was also a problem. Now I had put these men in a bad position, a position to be charged with sexual harassment. It was not expected of me to turn them down. I was supposed to be like the other females who did a little something to get a little something. Because I declined any offers, I was a threat, holding on to their little secrets.

They would do anything to get rid of me. My philosophy was, as long as I did my job, I was going to be all right.

I was raped twice while serving in the military, both by high-ranking individuals. One situation occurred while I was deployed. I reported it to no avail.

I was eventually investigated on the very thing that I had reported months prior. They had me investigated, being a suspect of an inappropriate relationship, adultery and a falsified statement. None of the above was true. I reported being harassed by the same man months prior. Nothing was done to protect me.

I never wrote a statement. I couldn't understand how they would try and charge me on that. Stupid I guess. This person was behaving inappropriately toward me. So there was no inappropriate relationship on my part.

They should have known that I was not going to fall for the okie doke. I had a clear knowledge of the investigation process. The investigating Officer did and said all of the wrong things. She was clueless. I was sort of embarrassed for her.

She tried to read to me my rights and have me write a sworn statement immediately afterwards. That was funny. I knew that I had to be presented with all of the evidence they had against me within a reasonable amount of time. The Regulation stated that a reasonable amount of time was five days. I had been presented with nothing.

I found out that day that I was supposed to meet with her, thirty minutes after the scheduled appointment.

I refused to sign anything. I requested to confer with an attorney. When I returned, I invoked my rights under the Article that provides me the right to remain silent. She had no clue of what that regulation was. She tried looking through her notes to figure out what I was saying to her.

After she attempted to continue questioning me, I politely explained to her the investigation process. I explained that after the invocation of my rights under said Article, she was no longer allowed to question me. I then politely requested to be dismissed.

That shook things up a bit around the Battalion. My leadership tried to coach me on what to write in my sworn statement. I knew that was wrong also. My intentions this time was not to fight the system. I only wanted to protect myself, and be left alone. They continued to dig a deeper hole.

I continued to document everything. I reported the reprisal and harassment that was to follow. I carefully establish my grounds just in case I had to fight.

They said that the investigation was in progress. Nevertheless, they had absolutely nothing. What evidence could they investigate other than the evidence that I was holding against the person harassing me. I refused to give them that, only because I had presented it to them prior, and they tried to make me the suspect to protect this leader. What they wanted or expected was for me to incriminate myself in a sworn statement. That's a negative.

Even sillier, this man tried contacted me through my leadership when he had absolutely nothing to do with me. If he had not contacted me, there would never have been any investigation.

Once I was cleared, the investigation turned on him, and I was the keeper of all the evidence against him. He put himself in a bad situation and no one thought about why he was trying to contact me. Once his investigation started, I began to receive threats; I made sure the leadership heard it for themselves.

I was told afterward that I was going to receive a letter of reprimand, not because I had done something wrong, but because something had to be turned in to higher. (Laughing) They really thought I was stupid. That was also a negative. I prepared myself for a fight. The Inspector General was going to have a nice fat packet of documentation on his desk by the next morning.

They left me alone.

The investigation backfired on the individuals who formed themselves against me[13] without just cause. I was the victim. I also had 2 years' worth of emails to prove the harassment. My case was tight. I could have countered the situation, but decided to request to be moved instead. It wasn't worth my sanity. I had already been diagnosed with PTSD. I did not need a trigger.

I knew then that I might not make it in this man's Army. Anything that looked like right was wrong. The things I suffered were all brushed under the rug to protect the reputation of the higher-ranking individual. I then became a victim of reprisal as well as rape.

I survived both.

---

[13] Isaiah 54:17 No weapon that is formed against thee shall prosper; and every tongue that shall rise against thee in judgment thou shalt condemn.

Not everyone in the military is to be blamed for the misbehavior of a few. Not everyone in the Army has had the same experiences that I have.

I am no recruiter, but the Army is a stepping-stone to the possibilities of a great future. I am proud to have served such a great Nation. I am proud to be an American Soldier. I have taken full responsibility for my part in a harsh beginning. I have learned many valuable lessons. I have also learned how to play the game without altering my moral standing.

It starts by simply forgiving. Forgiving those who have no clue of the pain they have caused. I also know that understanding plays a large role. Understanding that there is growth in every lesson learned. I also had my friend "Sister" by my side. There is no support like the support of a good friend.

I am certain that I will face many more perils while continuing to serve, but I am also determined to be a great leader, keeping the welfare of my soldiers uppermost in my mind.

The Army is strong and is becoming stronger. I will continue to serve faithfully until Uncle Sam releases me.

I have been taken places I never thought I would see in my lifetime. I have wandered on grounds that are considered Holy. I would not trade these experiences for the world. I would have nothing to write about without my life's experiences.

I have chosen my path from the beginning of time. I have humbly accepted my perils, my rises, and fallings. I have become a woman.

A POEM CALLED IN HIS IMAGE AND LIKENESS

BY GINA GENELLE

Under the shadow, I abide rendering the truths that your Lucifer hides,

I am the cries of the wise trapped in this physical being, Causing the demise of those watching without seeing

But again, I rise in the image you know as Christ, and all that it cost was the price of his life

I, the risen Sophia (Knowledge)

A percentage, my spirit lifted resurrected from within,

I am Gemini so I call her my twin.

I am the knowledge, the spoken Word, the third. Representing everything you know and heard

I won't bend, bow, or submit at all, you can build towers and temples or walls, but at the sound of His voice, every knee WILL fall.

*And it is written, bound to commence.
Recompense these souls, gotta let "em go,
and all that I am sayin' you already know*

*So incline your eyes for ears have not heard
the earthly manifestation of this spoken
Word.*

*I am that Light that darkness can't
comprehend, revealing your logic and
exposing the sin.*

*I have been told that my kingdom suffers
violence, and the violent taketh by force, so
let the powers that be take their course.*

Ready or not here I come

god
OR
GOD?
CHAPTER 11

DV8 (DEVIATE)

So, I assume it all seizes position in the book of Genesis. I assume this because it has always been taught in Sunday school and I have read its content for myself. Indeed, it says, "In the beginning."

So I ask, in the beginning of what? Does this mean the beginning of time? Does this mean the beginning of life, the beginning of earth?

The King James "version," thus, the word version, of the Holy bible states that in the beginning God created the heavens and the earth.

Correct me if I am wrong, but it also states that darkness was upon the face of the deep. I am sure that darkness as well as the deep is referred to in the text as separate things.

Now I am considering the words of the bible to be facts, and based on facts, there was never any mention of God creating neither the darkness nor the deep, which obviously had a face.

I am sure this face spoken of, means the contacting surface. So, again, I am compelled to ask, the beginning of what? Now I say that God created, but I am for certain that at some point God said "Let Us" Who is Us?[14] In fact, God said "Let us..." a couple of times that I can recall.

It is apparent that the darkness and the deep were present prior to creation of the earth, as I have always known it. There was definitely life and life forms prior to the creation of earth, which is obvious I know, but who is the god that we have been serving vs. the God we are to serve? Who is the God that created all other gods?

---

[14] Genesis 1:26 And God said, let us make man in our image. Genesis 11:7 Let us go down, and there confound their language.

The following Scriptures are scriptures that I have pulled together to give greater understanding of the way my journey to find God was manifested.

Genesis 1:26 And God said, let us make man in our image.
Genesis 3:22 And the Lord God said, Behold, then man is become as one of us, to know good and evil.
Genesis 11:7 Let us go down, and there confound their language.
Exodus 12:12 And against all the gods of Egypt I will execute judgment.
Exodus 15:11 Who is like unto thee, O LORD, among the gods?
Exodus 18:11 Now I know that the LORD is greater than all gods.
Exodus 20:3, 5 Thou shalt have no other gods before me. ... Thou shalt not bow down thyself to them, nor serve them.
Exodus 34:14 For thou shalt worship no other god: for the LORD, whose name is Jealous, is a jealous God.
Deuteronomy 5:7 Thou shalt have none other gods before me.
Deuteronomy 10:17 For the LORD your God is God of gods, and Lord of lords.

Joshua 24:2-14 They served other gods. (v.2) Fear the Lord ... and put away the gods which your fathers served. (v.14)

Judges 11:24 Wilt not thou possess that which Chemosh thy god giveth thee to possess?

I have said, Ye are gods. (v.6)

Psalm 96:4 For the Lord ... is to be feared above all gods.

Psalm 97:7 Worship him, all ye gods.

Psalm 135:5 Our Lord is above all gods.

Psalm 136:2 O give thanks unto the God of gods.

God Now we all know that God is not the author of confusion[15], so which of these god's have I been serving? Which was I suppose to be serving? I have read the bible through and through and so much of it was just not clicking with my spirit. I felt dead wrong for questioning the things that were vivid and undeniable. I needed desperately to figure this thing out. There were other scriptures that I found to be in direct conflict with the scriptures that I have just shared. I

---

[15] 1 Corinthians 14:33 For God is not the author of confusion, but of peace, as in all churches of the saints.

couldn't figure out what was going on, but I refused to discount God. I knew that God had been present most of my life and that was undeniable, but which one? Was it the God of Abraham, Isaac and Jacob? Was it the God of Moses? Which one?

Now take these scriptures into consideration

> Deuteronomy 4:35-39 Unto thee it was shewed, that thou mightest know that the LORD he is God; there is none else beside him. (v.35) The LORD he is God in heaven above, and upon the earth beneath: there is none else. (v.39)
> Deuteronomy 6:4 Hear, O Israel: The Lord our God is one Lord.
> Deuteronomy 32:39 See now that I, even I, am he, and there is no god with me.
> 1 Kings 18:39 The LORD, he is the God; the LORD, he is the God.
> Isaiah 43:10 I am he: before me there was no God formed, neither shall there be after me.
> Isaiah 44:8 I am the LORD, and there is none else ... There is none beside me. I am the LORD, and there is none else.

Isaiah 45:5-21 I am the Lord, and there is none else, there is no God beside me. (vv.5-6) There is no God else beside me ... There is none beside me. (v.21)

Isaiah 46:9 I am God, and there is none else: I am God, and there is none like me.

Mark 12:29-32 The Lord our God is one Lord. (v.29) There is one God; and there is none other but he. (v.32)

John 17:3 That they might know thee the only true God.

1 Corinthians 8:6 But to us there is but one God, the Father, of whom are all things, and we in him.

Contradiction!

Can you see it? What and who have I been serving? God or god? Lucifer has been loosely identified as the bearer of Light.[16] Man is dust made from dust, possessing the breath of life, given by the Almighty, or Us whoever Us is. The bible states that when a person dies the spirit goes back to the God that gave it[17], basically

---

[16] In Latin it's translated "Lucifer," light-bearer. Isaiah 14:12: "How art thou fallen from heaven, O Lucifer, son of the morning! How art thou cut down to the ground, which didst weaken the nations!"

[17] Ecclesiastes 12:7 "Then the dust returns to the earth (this is the body), and the Spirit returns to the God that gave it".

acknowledging that it is possible that there could be more than one creation. Not verbatim but that is what it says. So does this mean that it is possible that I was correct in thinking that something was not right in that church?

During the tarrying services where there was constant chanting in hopes of receiving the Holy Ghost, could this have been the time where people were invoking the spirit of the bearer of the light?

We sang a song in church all the time. It said,

"I know God is a good God, yes he is, I know God is a good God, yes he is, he's the Lilly in the valley, yes he, he's my bright and morning star, yes he is"

Hmm...He is my bright and morning star. Did anyone else catch that? Whom have we been serving? Not only that, but if God is a good God, does that mean there are bad gods?

Lucifer was given charge of the earth, thus becoming the god of this world. He is known as the bright and morning star. 2 Corinthians 4:4 states, "In whom the god of this world hath blinded the minds of them which believe not, lest the light of the glorious gospel of Christ, who is the image of God, should shine unto them." He was the bearer of the one true Light. He was the one who was cast out of heaven taking a third with Him.

Isaiah 14:12, How you have fallen from heaven, O morning star, son of the dawn! You have been cast down to the earth, you who once laid low the nations! 13 You said in your heart, "I will ascend to heaven; I will raise my throne above the stars of God; I will sit enthroned on the mount of assembly, on the utmost heights of the sacred mountain. I will ascend above the tops of the clouds; I will make myself like the Most High."

The bible never said that he lost his power and also describes a moment where he was given power by God to persuade a righteous man (JOB)[18]. He was spoken of to be beautiful, appealing to the eye, just like the fruit of the tree of knowledge of good and evil.

Ezekiel 28:12 .."`You were the model of perfection, full of wisdom and perfect in beauty. 13 You were in Eden, the garden of God; every precious stone adorned you: ruby, topaz and emerald, chrysolite, onyx and jasper, sapphire, [2] turquoise and beryl. [3] Your settings and mountings [4] were made of gold; on the day you were created they were prepared. 14 You were anointed as a guardian cherub, for so I ordained you. You were on the holy mount of God; you walked among the fiery stones. 15 You were blameless in your ways from the day you were created till wickedness was found

---

[18] Job 1:10-12 Hast not thou made an hedge about him, and about his house, and about all that he hath on every side? thou hast blessed the work of his hands, and his substance is increased in the land. But put forth thine hand now, and touch all that he hath, and he will curse thee to thy face. And the LORD said unto Satan, Behold, all that he hath is in thy power; only upon himself put not forth thine hand. So Satan went forth from the presence of the LORD.

in you. 16 Through your widespread trade you were filled with violence, and you sinned. So I drove you in disgrace from the mount of God, and I expelled you, O guardian cherub, from among the fiery stones. 17 Your heart became proud on account of your beauty, and you corrupted your wisdom because of your splendor. So I threw you to the earth; I made a spectacle of you before kings.

Could it have been possible that we already possessed the knowledge of good and Lucifer introduced evil, explaining that Adam and Eve would become like god, referring to himself, the one who possessed evil? Could it be that this was purposed for a greater plan?

I have heard tale that there was human life prior to the creation of Adam and Eve. Could it be possible that the verse in Genesis that states, "Let Us make man in Our image and likeness" it could have been Lucifer speaking to his fallen angels, patterning new life form after him, possessing the spirit of iniquity? This would explain a man's spirit returning unto the God that gave it.

Though this new form of man or mankind, still having a choice, they now possessed iniquity. Could it be possible that Lucifer's angels shielded the tree of life? Could he have tried to hide truth from Adam and Eve. Or did God's angels shield the tree of live, protecting Adam and Eve from partaking of the tree of life while in a sinful nature, protecting them from eternal life in a sinful state.

LETS JUST SAY THIS WERE TRUE

Let's take Cain and Abel. Abel offered a sincere offering to God and it reached heaven. Cain was vain and offered vanity. With the same envy in his heart that his god (Lucifer) possessed, he became enraged and killed his brother when he was praised for his good deed[19]. (today's modern society would call Cain a hater)

God Almighty was disappointed at Cain's choices and set out to chastise him. Cain complained of his punishment, and his god came to his rescue, cursing anyone that so much as touched a hair on Cain's head. It sounds like Cain had been rewarded for his mischievous

---

[19] Genesis 4:13 Cain said to the Lord, "My punishment is more than I can bear. 14 Today you are driving me from the land, and I will be hidden from your presence; I will be a restless wanderer on the earth, and whoever finds me will kill me." 15 But the Lord said to him, "Not so[e]; anyone who kills Cain will suffer vengeance seven times over." Then the Lord put a mark on Cain so that no one who found him would kill him. 16 So Cain went out from the Lord's presence and lived in the land of Nod,[f] east of Eden.

behavior, or maybe protected because at this time, there was no law, and without law, how can a man sin?

Also, the bible says that god is a jealous god. That to me also sounds like the characteristics of Lucifer.

This is simply my thought process, not to be confused with fact. I am not encouraging anyone to believe in this manner. Just an attempt to encourage individuals to study to show thyself approved.

I dare not persuade anyone to follow or believe as I do, I just pray that these things are considered when giving my account of the journey that brought me to a real God

There is a great difference (I cannot stress this enough) between TRUTH and truths. That is what the enemy gets us on. Who is the enemy? Ourselves!

All power is in the mind and in the tongue. We speak what we think. God spoke the world into existence and we are created in His image and likeness, so we are natural creators. We utilize words as a vessel to carry the faith that creates our desires. We sometimes create things that are not as desirable. I know you've heard the terms "Be careful of what you wish for", "Watch what you say" or "You spoke that into existence". Well, those are natural creations. It works. I said I was going to write a successful book. Well, here is my book and I believe that it will be successful, even if it just touches 1 life.

The bible tells us not to be conformed to the things of this world, but transformed by the renewing of our minds. I am no bible scholar, and I will not pretend to be, but I have studied to show myself approved. I live according to the simplicity of the gospel so to speak.

Now here are the meat and potatoes.

I was lying on my sofa one evening; I had just put my bible down. I had been studying and considering Moses. I was trying to truly understand what was really taking place. God hardened the heart of Pharaoh. This was very odd.

Moses said unto God, "Behold, when I come unto the children of Israel, and shall say to them, The God of your fathers have sent me unto you; and they will say to me, What is his name? What shall I say to them? And God said unto Moses, " I AM THAT I AM", and he said, "You shall say unto the children of Israel, "I AM" has sent me unto you."

I put my bible down and asked God..."what is your name? Lord I know that you have been with me throughout my life, but who are you? What God has been with me all this time?" I was scared to present this question to God; after all, His name was not to be utilized in vain. I picked up the bible and began to search again for the name of God, I was seeking to be led by His spirit. Lo and behold, I stumbled across this scripture...

Psalms 9:10 - And they that know thy name will put their trust in thee: for thou, LORD, hast not forsaken them that seek thee.

I started now to search harder. I was determined. I started to research the names of God in Judaism, hoping to find the God that had been with me.

El (One of the oldest names of a monotheistic God, dating at least as early as tablets found in Syria 2300 BC)
Elohim ("Strong One" or "Lord Almighty")
Ehyeh-Asher-Ehyeh ("I am that I am")
Adonai ("My Lord" and origin of the Greek name Adonis)
YHWH
El Shaddai ("Almighty" According to Exodus 6:2, 3, Shaddai was the name by which God was known to Abraham, Isaac and Jacob.)
Zebaot ("Heavenly Host")

I found that Christians recognize names of God, but none seem to truly match what I found in Judaism. They both recognized seven names for God.

    YHWH-Yireh "The Lord will provide" (Genesis 22:13-14)
    YHWH-Rapha "The Lord that healeth" (Exodus 15:26)

    YHWH-Niss"i "The Lord our Banner" (Exodus 17:8-15)
    YHWH-Shalom "The Lord our Peace" (Judges 6:24)
    YHWH-Ra-ah "The Lord my Shepherd" (Psalm 23:1)

    YHWH-Tsidkenu "The Lord our Righteousness" (Jeremiah 23:6)
    YHWH-Shammah "The Lord is present" (Ezekiel 48:35)

This was confusing me even more. They all seemed to be titles as opposed to names. So I put my bible and laptop down and decided to just pray. I prayed all night long, in and out of my sleep, requesting that God would reveal his name to me. As day began to break, I began to utter a word...Ehyeh! And again, Ehyeh! Repeatedly, Ehyeh, Ehyeh, Ehyeh followed by Asher Ehyeh. I was familiar with the sound of what I was uttering, but continued without disturbance. Ehyeh Asher Ehyeh, I called out with tears in my eyes, because I remembered that these words translated meant I AM THAT I AM. I AM THAT I AM. And without doubt, I knew that God had provided me with the answer that I sought...I AM THAT I AM. This was the same God that presented Himself to Moses, when Moses requested His name. I had found my God, a real God. The real God! God was, is and will be ALL THINGS.

HERE ARE MY TRUTHS

God is as great as you believe Him to be. Faith!

God simply cannot exist to you if you don't allow it. We are the creators of our gods. God Almighty, the Light just is, with or without us. Where is He? He is in my mind, spirit, body and soul! He is in the very breath of me.

I believe that the bible holds enough guidance for us to obtain the true knowledge and wisdom of truth.

I believe that the bible was tampered with to force subordinate people to conform to a standard that society could handle, and be handled. (thus versions)

My personal wrong or right is determined by me, with the commandments utilized as only a mediator. I have been given a choice, and because of the natural wickedness within me, I have been provided a redeemer. Christ…But My idea of Christ is the black men and women with hair as nappy as mine. Sacrificing their live by hanging from trees by their necks. I cannot find the passion in just one white man and ignore the millions of my ancestors who suffered way worse. I just cannot relate to a blonde hair blue eyed savior. I prayed that I am understood without being thought of as racist. I am not. I just can't relate to something that I am not familiar with. I DO NOT HATE anyone. I just don't believe a white person is my savior.

I was created to be the righteousness of God, having a created body, built to house His spirit.

I believe that God is a spiritual force, ineffable, the very breath in my body, a source of energy, LIGHT. He is attributes, the universe, He is all things.

I believe that Lucifer is also powerful. He often presenting himself as an angel of Light, created also by God. I believe he is an attribute of God, divided, as was the darkness from the Light.

I believe that there is a battle in the spiritual realm that we humans manifest in the physical through thoughts and the creations of our minds.

I believe that both good and bad spiritual aspects of being influence everything that is manifested in this physical world.

I believe that we are natural creators. As a man thinketh, so is he.

If Christ is not real, I choose to believe in him. He is my example. The Way, the Truth, and the Light. Well written to say the least. I choose to exercise my faith and believe.

I believe that the bible holds many mysteries.

I believe the earth is flat…there, I said it

I believe that he who has an ear will hear, and understand the Knowledge with a clear understanding.

God or no God, it is my choice. I believed the name and idea of God was created by man to better pinpoint our belief in something that is there, but not visible. Our faith, which is the substance of things hoped for, and the evidence of things not seen is what allows God to exist for the believer. Like air, we cannot see it but know that it is there. We call it air to better identify the unexplained, a form of control, a creation, a balance. We understand the characteristic of air, but like God, it is unexplainable. We also could not explain the source of bad, iniquity, wickedness, or evil so we give it a source.

We name it Satan, Lucifer, Devil or demonic force, just as we associate good, love, divine, blessed, holy, and heavenly with the source we named God. But the word says that God created evil.

Isaiah 45:7 I form the light, and create darkness: I make peace, and create evil: I the Lord do all these things.

We understand that it/he, Lucifer also is created by God, (our dictionaries made by man, call God a thing of power) which means evil came from God, created perfectly evil. God makes no mistakes.

We accept and magnify stories of Lucifer's fall to rid God of any association of evil. We are the middle ground, the determining factor. The center of what we choose to believe, right or wrong.

We disregard the possibility that it and we are all ONE, all from one source or thing of power. God.

I choose to believe in Christ, and Him crucified. I believe he is truly the son of God, as we are adopted unto the father as we enter into the knowledge of truth. That is my truth. It is what leads me to the Way, the Truth, and the Light. Christ was an example of what we are and are to become.

As said in congress, I hold MY truths to be Self- evident. No one has to accept it for fact.

I am the center balance. I am what lie between true and false. I am the center of the universe. My choice is what determines truth, my truth.

I am the meeting point between Ying and Yang. I am the shortest distance between the two points that divides the darkness from the Light. I am the medium between night and day. I am sin and repentance. I possess the power to forgive. Forgiveness of my personal sin is not, unless I accept that I have been forgiven by others.

Without one of anything the other simply cannot exist. Pay attention to how many times the word divided is used in Genesis. Divide is to separate into opposites. In order to divide something it has to first be one whole.

I am North-East, East-South, South-West, and West-North, the deviation from paths and direction chosen for me.

I am my past, present and future. I am the body of the source of creation, the body that holds the breath of life.

I am the contradiction as well as the contradistinction. I am control. I am contempt, forthright, and I am vicarious. I am bad and good, choosing to partake of the latter.

I am Wisdom.

I am captivity as well as freedom.

I am palindrome words uttered. I am misunderstood and understood. I am unimportant and important.

I am that I am.

I cannot answer for everyone, but have concluded for myself. I understand my power and spiritual authority. I know where my source comes from. I have battled so much with what is right or wrong, based on someone else's teachings or thoughts on life. I have tried to live according to someone else's rules, unsuccessfully. I have been a prisoner to what I felt society deemed right and wrong.

A prisoner to how I should wear my hair, what I should not do as a woman, what clothes I should where, whom I should or should not date, or I shouldn't date at all. What church I should attend, who I should love, what race I am, what job I should have, what car I should drive, what neighborhood I should live in, what social clubs I should attend and so on.

In the end, it is all vanity. Will I take it with me when this physical body perishes? Where should my treasures lie? When this body is gone, does my spirit have a second chance at it in new flesh?

I was a prisoner being held hostage. I was a P.O.W, (Prisoner of War) but my war was of the mind. I was enslaved with no shackles, no cuffs, and no bars. I was imprisoned by my mind. I could not free myself from the constraint of my own knowledge persuaded by others. I needed to be free from me.

There is another passage in the bible, it states that we need not be entangle again in the yoke of bondage from which we have been made free. Why do we continually bind ourselves?

I am a self-thinker. I have finally found my freedom.

My choice! My will! My question to you is... Have you found yours?

Naked

Naked

I am naked.

I have nothing to cover me but the perishable design that holds the content of my person.

This life began for me in its purest form, naked and unknowing. I entered into a state of being called life.

Within me were all the attributes of existing, to include perceived perfection as well as iniquity. The two made me whole. The essence of every possibility resided with in me, powered by the breath of life. I am reminded of that power with each breath taken.

As I begin to grow, people offered me knowledge of good and evil, and I became a partaker of the same. I began to deny a part of my physical and spiritual make up. I was given instructions on what was considered wrong or right. I began to tear myself down based on another person's conclusion. I tried to divide myself from myself.

With this knowledge of good and evil, I began to separate self from self. I realized that I was naked and developed a strong desire to cover myself. I did not want anyone to know or see who I really was. I did not want to see for myself who I really was.

I did not want the world to know that I was bad even if I had not exercised it. I only wanted to be judged based upon the positive attributes of self. I wanted to be praised for a job well done, ignoring a part of me that will never go away.

Because of my knowledge of good and evil, I wanted to rid myself of the iniquity. I did not want to own any parts of the wickedness that resided within me. I wanted nothing to do with a piece of myself that ultimately made me who I am.

I hid myself from God. I tried to hide from Him what was obvious to Him. I separated myself from God, who is the creator of all things and is all things. I wanted all of God, with the exception of one part of him, the part that I deemed unworthy. I judged God. God is now asking, just as He asked Adam, Gina where are you?

Society and religion places such great emphasis on right and wrong. So many laws and commandments govern what is acceptable and what is not.

It had only taught me self-hate. These rules and regulations have only taught me to deny who I am.

I am not saying that I should take the opportunity to rehearse negativity. I am simply stating that I should never have attempted to mortify my personal opposition. It is I. I could never be whole if part of me has been cast down.

This knowledge of good and evil is the most wicked device known to man. It causes hate, separation, and judgment. It hinders people from accepting the grace of God due to constant condemnation and bondage[20]. That bondage becomes a form of control for others to carry over our head. God understood our nature, which is why He gave up Jesus.

Knowledge of good and evil is the insecurity of a young teenage girl, so insecure that she takes her life.

This knowledge is the fist of a man who pounds the face of the woman he claims to love dearly, because he feels that he is inadequate and not good enough for her.

It is the demise of a race of people because of the color of their skin or religious preference.

It is the separation of us from God.

---

[20] Galatians 5:1 Stand fast therefore in the liberty wherewith Christ hath made us free, and be not entangled again with the yoke of bondage.

If a young girl had no knowledge of what is perceived as beauty, she would have never had a basis on which to judge herself so harshly. She would never have chosen a permanent solution to a temporary problem. She would have cherished the inevitable part of her. The part that she assumed the world considered ugly.

One life lost in efforts to cover her nakedness.

An insecure man beats the face of his lover because he feels that she has an interest in another man. A man that he feels he could never be compared with. He has already thrown out the possibilities of his inner beauty because of his knowledge of good and evil, now with that very same knowledge, he is crucially judged by the world as an abusive man. He utilized the same knowledge to negatively judge himself compared to a man who may have held the same insecurity.

We use clothing to cover our bodies. We fear the exposing of our being naked. We point fingers when a person wears clothing that exposes skin. We call them smutty or loose.

This is exactly what we do to our inner man. We create ways to cover the part of us that is considered unacceptable. Clothing can only cover what will continue to exist without fail.

No one wants to be naked. We will cast stones at anyone who is comfortable with being naked. I am meaning naked in the physical as well as mental sense of the word. But most importantly, Spiritually naked and without the coat of skin that God provided us with

Life has found a way to accept anything other than its true nature. Life becomes an impossible task when the chore of declining your true nature is added.

When I was a little girl, I wandered around half- naked, literally, but totally naked mentally and spiritually. My mind was completely free of judgment. I did not judge myself, nor did I judge others. I lived life happily.

In church with my Great grandmother, I shouted to please her. I was not admired for my innocence. I was admired for what they thought was praising God. My people pleasing started in church. It is my first memory. The moment I began to be separate from God, separated from my true nature. I was exposed to the knowledge of good and evil in church.

No matter how bad life was for me, while wandering, I was free. I loved me and acknowledged all the possibilities that life had to offer. I was not imprisoned by denouncing myself. I loved me. It did not matter how nappy headed or dirty I was. I was free to live and learn. I chose without thought to behave righteously. It felt right. No one ever had to tell me.

I ate of the tree of life freely.

I do not want anyone to misunderstand and assume that I am saying do what you want to do, good or bad, I am simply saying, love yourself, good or bad. Accept who you are. We still must abide by the laws of the land.

It started with me, not conforming to the things of this world, but being transformed by the renewing of my mind[21].

The mind is life's playground. It all starts in our minds. We create our images of God. We create our images of the devil. It is all a figment of our imaginations stemming from our true inner being, good and evil. It is all

---

[21] Romans 12:2 And be not conformed to this world: but be ye transformed by the renewing of your mind, that ye may prove what is that good, and acceptable, and perfect, will of God.

one. We create the divide as God divided the darkness from the Light, as above, so below.

When we become one with ourselves, it is then that the body is edified. We are enlightened. I am not saying I am God, nor will I say that my daughter is I, but it is the same difference. She came from me. She and I were one until the divide.

Today I am naked. I have exposed myself to the world. I have embraced me. I am becoming one with myself again and building a relationship with the creator of all. I have been illuminated. I have found God. One, all in all.

Let he who has an ear, hear...

My aunt died 4 years after this book was published. I am grateful that she understood why I needed to write this book. Because of her, I learned one of life's most valuable lessons. To forgive and be forgiven.

Rest in Peace Ainty

Proverbial Evolution

Taking the Blame for My Own Fall By
Gina Genelle

COMING SOON!

Proverbial Evolution

Taking the Blame for Mistakes I Didn't
Even Commit

COMING SOON!

Proverbial Evolution

Thanks for worrying about me, but are you concerned for your own soul at all?

I am a big girl now, and I can take the blame for my own fall.

I laugh at how I have memorized the patterns and groves in your fingertips and have remembered the methods of movements in your lips when fixed to spew judgment upon me.

And I appreciate that you would be so concerned for the saving of my soul, that you would let your own go to make me a better person.

Thank you, I have become the woman that you wanted me to be, you can let go now, I am setting you free.

Now that I am an adult, I will take the blame for my own fall.

I will own my own responsibility and maintain me, so that you can see.

Now that you have fixed me, you remain broken. And with the word repeatedly spoken through your voice, you forgot to live it as well as teach.

Excited about the weekend that you are scheduled to preached.

Practicing your message, forgetting to ask God to bless it.

Self-motivated, concentrated on the sound and how profound this speech will be.

Why wasn't there ever God in it? It took me a minute, but I am no longer in need of guidance of that sort.

And if by chance I fall short. I will take the blame for my own fall.

-Gina Genelle

www.ingramcontent.com/pod-product-compliance
Lightning Source LLC
Chambersburg PA
CBHW070847050426
42453CB00012B/2078